MW01087211

The Birthing Hour

by

Tony Whitman

Sage & Hawthorn Print, LLP

Cover photograph of Tony and Thales copyright © 2010 by Jessica Tiderman

Copyright © 2013 by Tony Whitman
All rights reserved. This book or any portion thereof
may not be reproduced or used in any manner whatsoever
without the express written permission of the publisher
except for the use of brief quotations in a book review.

Printed in the United States of America

Second Printing, 2014

ISBN 978-0-615-92122-8

Sage & Hawthorn Print, LLP
www.sagehawthorn.com

Dedication

My eternal thanks to Michelle Loring, Jer Walker, and Erin Riley for their overwhelming support and their help with the editing and proofreading process.

My love to my wife, Jessica Tiderman, who is the one who put me on this path that to have the experience and desire to write this book.

Contents

Chapter One
Current Situation

Saturday Afternoons

Situation One: It is a sunny day and a history channel is airing its usual mix of alien astronaut, Hitler, and reality shows. The dog is snoring in the sunbeam on the floor. Dinner doesn't have to be made for two more hours. Then the wife, four months into her first pregnancy, casually walks by the husband and mentions that she wants her first birth to be a home birth.

Situation Two: It's a rainy day and the rabbit cages need cleaned. The kids are having leftovers for dinner. There is a good movie on about zombies and viruses. In this scenario, the wife walks up to the husband and informs him that even though the last pregnancy was horrible and she still feels pain in her cesarean scar – she wants to have the next child as a vaginal birth.

Situation Three: It's another day at the office. So far, this doctor has treated three toddlers with colds and an elderly woman with severe arthritis. After two more appointments, it is time for lunch at some fast food place down the street. During the drive, his wife calls and asks him how he feels about having their next child at a birth center with a midwife, and not the hospital where he works.

The first person is totally unprepared. This is his first birth. He hasn't read anything at all on pregnancy, let alone the medical knowledge he might need for a home birth. None of his family members or friends have told him stories about their own deliveries. He isn't even sure how much he should be involved, if at all, when his wife goes into labor.

The emotionally scarred father in the second situation feels that he does not have the emotional resolve to relive the trauma that may come if the delivery is difficult. He is still coping with seeing her on the operating table. No one discussed with him how to help his wife deal with the post-partum depression that sometimes occurs after a drastic change in a birth plan.

Lastly, the doctor doesn't know how he will tell his boss that his wife is having her child at a birthing center. He may not be ready for the medical ostracism that he may face at work. Some of his co-workers might feel offended that the birth isn't happening at their hospital. He may not want to risk his career for his wife's wishes.

These examples aren't representative of all the situations in which fathers-to-be may find themselves in. They do not reveal the entire spectrum of best-to-worst case scenarios. What these situations do is demonstrate how helpless the fathers are to deal with the change presented. They do not know how to prepare for the new situation.

While one of these situations may be more or less likely than another, they all have one constant: a woman who wants a different birthing experience which puts the father in a new and alien position. These types of requests have become very commonplace. For various reasons, women have decided to take a more assertive role in determining how and where their births take place. As the next logical step, those same women have also decided that they want their partners more involved in their choice of birth plans. Whenever I speak of the birth partner or father-to-be; it is not meant to refer to men only. Some birth partners are family members, the significant other in a same sex relationship, or friends. Even though special consideration for the biological father may seem apparent – the resulting dialogue can include any type of birth partner that the mother may desire.

Unfortunately, the supply of resources has not kept up with the new flurry of these demands. The materials and resources for the men previously described are being developed at almost a crawl, if at all. Is there a conventional wisdom upsurge or publishing binge to fill this void? Are there places that fathers who wish to be included as much as possible in the birth can turn to? Are there any standards or role models that normal and everyday fathers can ponder, rely on, or transform into their own personal mold? No.

Of course, there are fathers out there who did have the luck or strength to overcome these described scenarios and many other possibilities. Those who met new situations head on are the exception to the rule. Unfortunately, fathers in the western world do not exist in societies that encourage the passing on of their experience to others. Most parents had to develop the father's role completely from scratch. This issue also needs to be confronted.

The goal of this book is to address the absence of dialogue, and the lack of freedom for birth partners to find their own niche during labor. We can take steps to further open the social dialogue and expose the desire for couples to help fathers fully reach their potential. An intellectual revolution resulting in laboring women having truly unique and useful birth partners cannot be viewed as a negative end result. Those who have an entrenched, narrow, and absolute view of the father's place during birth – either totally involved or completely removed – will not enjoy this book. People who know that roles have varied throughout history and would enjoy comparing and contrasting their favorite approaches, as well as develop their own, will enjoy this journey immensely.

This book seeks to arm those who wish to be a more progressive partner in the labor with information. A father who fears snide glances or lengthy lectures at family holidays can offer a short response of how the Roman paterfamilias had a legal right to kill his own newborn sons. A doctor who fears ostracism from co-workers can talk about two nurses in England who had no problems with their own home birth. Any person who would try to argue that there is any standard attitude, let alone not consider various options, cannot hold any type of sway over the person who has studied the topic of fathers at birth from multiple viewpoints.

What will not be found here are birth stories, scapegoating, medical jargon, or self-help terminology. I will try to keep the statistics and biology terminology to a minimum. What will be presented is a clear examination of the roles and challenges of fatherhood - sometimes historical, sometimes philosophical, but always concise.

When the term birth is used throughout this book – it refers to some preparation during the pregnancy for the labor, the actual delivery, and also a short time after the child is born. For the sake of brevity, the term birth is sufficient.

For many reasons today, a few fathers are not involved in births; of those who are, many feel unsure or unsatisfied with their role. Entire books exist on the importance of fathers at birth and are numerous in the areas of family statistics, psychological evaluations, sociological theories, anthropological instances, etc. Yes, both parents should be there, but what should the role and function of the father be? We know the why, but not the how. My chief concern is informed choice for the fathers in the development of these much needed roles.

There may be a few crude individuals who would say that a father has no place in the birth process. The only reply that would suffice would be just as crude. If men were not needed, then women would be asexual! This book will not waste much time and effort addressing the people who hold this stance. A more positive and higher standard must be set. Focus must be on examining the participation of fathers in the past and present, as well as the possibilities of rebuilding and re-examining the development of more involved roles for the father.

It would be hypocritical for me to ask other fathers to think seriously about their own roles without having thought about and presented mine. If someone has to take the initiative and speak first – I will gladly be one of those leaders. I don't talk about myself in the hopes of persuading others to think like me, but to set an example of how to think for one's self. Hopefully, this won't count as a birth story, and will be the only time I get close to that line!

My language may get dry and lofty at times, but I am no doctor or professor. To start with - I was a high school jock. I spent a few young adult years moving around the country partying like many my age while working factory jobs. After shuffling around a bit, I settled down, spent 5 years getting a bachelor's degree, got married, and had two kids, all while still working random factory and security jobs. My life is nothing special. I am lucky in that my wife is very passionate about birth studies, and it rubbed off on me.

My wife decided to have our second child as an unassisted home birth. That wasn't a complete shock to me, as our first child was born in a freestanding birth center. Both times, we tried to find anything that would help me prepare for these types of birth. After our second birth, the memory of the giant void of resources aimed at the birth partner caught my interest.

I have an average sized library, four or five shelves of random books about history, old college textbooks, some classics, as well as some philosophy books. Out of curiosity, I went through all my books looking for any references to birth, let alone men and birth. I was not trying to set myself up for disappointment, but just wanted to see how far the void went. Interestingly enough, the only discussions on the topic in my library were found in a textbook from a Greek Mythology class offered at the local university. The books on mythology, and another on the daily life of ancient Greece did have a few paragraphs about the role of fathers in life and myth. (Listed in the bibliography.)

Naturally, I got online and scoured the Internet for books that may have changed my opinion that there isn't much out there for fathers and birth, in any field or study. I did manage to find a few books in which information on this topic could be gleaned. The void of direct resources bordered on truth. Luckily, my wife had a book called *Father for Life: A Journey of Joy, Challenge, and Change*, by Armin Brott. In the very first sentence of the first chapter, he states, "Until fairly recently, there has been precious little research on the expectant father's emotional and psychological experiences during pregnancy." This book was published in 2003.

In the dozen or more books I found directed at fathers about birth, there were patterns, so much so that I decided that there should be a whole chapter devoted to what these books have to say and how they say it. Even though there will be a bibliography section at the end, I felt it would be beneficial to review these books on their content relating to birth alone. I will not judge them in their entirety, but only analyze what they have to say about the very short window of actual childbirth.

There were very few books that dealt only with the exploration of how fathers think and what they should do during labor. There were a few collections of birth stories by fathers. Almost all of them were preparations for the nine months of pregnancy, extremely brief descriptions of the three stages of labor, and advice for the first two years of the infant's life.

Family Holidays

One day, when I was talking with my father about what was in the few birth books out there for dads, he casually mentioned that he had taken Lamaze classes and held my mother's hand and helped her during labor. He also stated that he was considered part of the first generation of fathers allowed in the room during labor (I was born in 1978). My father was a labor coach by today's standards. My face went blank with confusion. Why had he waited until after my children were born to talk about his own experiences?

The exploration of the differing roles that fathers or birth partners want during labor is not part of our dialogue. Clear examples can be made about what fathers and their sons talk about, and what they don't. In relation, some things in life can be avoided, others cannot. For example, death is inevitable. Some fathers talk to their sons about death, some don't. On the flip side, many things in life are avoidable, but that still doesn't stop that dialogue from happening. Not all sons go to college, but many fathers still talk to their young sons about it as if they would go. What I'm saying is that there are many types of dialogue out there between fathers and sons about things that may or may not happen. For some reason, birth is not included in these examples of dialogue.

Preparation is usually the key goal of these conversations. There are even stereotypes out there. We have all seen or heard of a father teaching his son how to fix a car. We know about fathers who teach their sons how to hunt, dress animals, clean a fish, etc. Has anyone ever heard of, or seen, a father preparing his son for birth? There are always exceptions to the rule, but it is still clear that pregnancy and labor talks don't exactly fall into the same category as cars and fishing. We know that people have examined sports from gladiators down to modern football, but very few have examined the fathers' roles in birth. The ones that did focused on very specific periods of history. I am not the only one who sees this as a shocking revelation. I found another author who had made the same observation: "Men in the United States do not learn about birth from their fathers around the campfire, nor do they watch other dads in the delivery room. They do not generally talk about it over beer or basketball. In fact, men are not much of a source of information for birthing fathers. When experienced dads do talk to young fathers about birth, their advice is usually supportive, but perfunctory; as one put it, "The one friend I talked with said my part is to stay on my feet where she can see me."[1]

To me, this seems like a stark contradiction. Hunting, fishing, sports, college, cars – these are all things that may or may not happen in a person's life. Birth however, is almost universal. I look at my son and have a feeling that the probability of him having kids is very high. I don't know if he will like sports or go to college. In our modern society, it's even getting to the point that homosexual couples are expected to have kids just as heterosexual couples are. Luckily for all adoptive fathers, Armin Brott has some good advice on the stages that adoptive fathers go through. How this dialogue is not given much, if any, attention seems to border on the absurd to many, including me.

This lack of care given to the preparation for fathers at birth becomes very apparent when reality rears its huge head. I first became aware of this reality while my wife was trying to navigate the myriad of available options of where and how to give birth to our first child, even though it was her fourth. Not having any preparation for this facet, let alone the intricacies of the birth itself, may stop fathers from developing clear roles before the process can even begin.

It must also be stated here that the brief historical examinations presented in this book take place in patriarchal societies. There really is no need to go into the why – as it doesn't start to change until the present day, nor does it change the truths discussed in the past. It is worth mentioning that one would think that discussions between men about birth would be more likely in patriarchal societies, but the fact that this isn't the case is about as far as the patriarchal observation takes us.

It will also be taken as a given that women want their birth partners involved to varying degrees. I did not feel it necessary to compile quotes from women who say they want their husbands or birth partners involved. It is also a given, and we will not go into the fact that there are varying degrees that fathers and birth partners

[1] Reed, Richard K. *Birthing Fathers: The Transformation of Men in American Rites of Birth.* (New Brunswick: Rutgers University Press, 2005), 135.

want to be involved during delivery. Even after all new and old considerations, there will be men who still want to simply wait outside, some who want to take classes and be a coach, some who want to be the sole person there, and some who remain aloof and just go through whatever motions will keep his wife content. This book is for the discussion of those who want to have an active role, not the judgment of those persons who don't.

Having stated the case, I decided to start from scratch. I wanted to start at the beginning, the roots of our western culture, Ancient Greece. I found and used examples from related cultures throughout history that weren't always American. The random references discussed were not my choice, as I had to work with what research was available, which was little. Some points in time are from the history of the United Kingdom, Rome, Australia, and Europe in general.

The cultural focus may be confusing at times. I am speaking from the experience of an American. However, I am drawing from Western sources and examples such as British and Australian ones. The lack of guidance for fathers and birth is applicable to most cultures and societies in the Western World, regardless of the different reasons and the method of information dissemination to all relevant cultures. It is possible for specific cultures or societies lacking in this field of discussion to learn from the American model presented here. There are also differences in laws in the United Kingdom, Australia, Italy, France, etc.

I was the person presented in scenario one. My wife wanted to have our first child born at a birthing center – regardless of her past cesareans, one of which was an Inverted T, which is an unusual cesarean incision. After that uncomplicated delivery, we decided that our second should be unassisted at home. Some may argue with me on this point, but I believe that the mother first chooses the type of birth she wants to have. She may take considerations from the father into account, but ultimately, the decision is hers alone. Once that choice is made, it is then the father's choice to decide his role in that birth. The secondary decision of our function and level of involvement can still have a tremendous impact.

I learned a lot sharing birth-related discoveries and experiences with my wife. I want to pass on the wisdom gained. In essence – the lack of materials and resources forced me to examine my plot – which led to further musings on the grand scale and scope of the father's designs around childbirth. There is little modern research, and even less that delves into the methods of fathers in the past. Fathers now have the chance to recognize and accept that hole in our identity, get our bearings, and change this unacceptable status quo. We need to start demanding and supplying the proper resources: literature, dialogues, and research - for the full development of our roles during the birthing hour.

Chapter Two
Conflicting Opinions

The Machine that goes Ping!

My wife decided to have her fifth child as an unassisted birth after cesarean or UBAC for those in the know. Our son was born according to plan, both nature's and ours; however, the placenta did not come out when it in a timely manner. After a certain amount of time, I called 911. The local, (meaning our little small town) paramedics arrived and as soon as the male EMTs saw my wife and baby, they put two and two together. They immediately turned around and went out to the ambulance to get the sole woman in the squad.

The point here is not to overburden the reader with anecdotes and inside jokes, but to lead in to very relevant questions. Were the EMTs unsure of what to do next? Did they feel that they were not qualified to make decisions affecting a birthing woman? Did they think it was immodest of them to help a woman in so sacred a position? I can't answer these questions. The important observation is how they did not take control of the situation and instead retrieved the only female EMT. It was simply instinctive.

When my wife was transferred to the hospital, I actually asked the nurses and OB in the emergency room: "Where is the machine that goes ping?" To my surprise, no one understood the joke. Understanding the joke is the same as describing the current situation concerning fathers, (and men in general, like the EMTs,) and birth in the best way - no other description comes nearly as close as the delivery room scene in the Monty Python movie, *The Meaning of Life*. One of the doctors tells the father, "I'm sorry, only those involved are allowed in here."

The true tragedy is that, more than twenty years later, that comedic scene is not too far from the current norm in most hospitals. Fathers are usually allowed in the delivery room now, but they are only *tolerated*. They are not expected by most hospitals to serve any real function other than that of a witness, or at most, a labor coach. They are usually simply invisible.

I would like to state that the intention here is not to vilify hospitals and blame them for all the ills of parenthood. It is very unlikely that in every hospital, there is an administrator who wakes up every morning and tells themselves that it is their personal duty to keep all men home and as far away as possible from their wives during labor, although some people out there may even argue this point.

The current standard is that birth partners have to fight, some with much less resistance than others, for the right to have active roles before, during, and after childbirth. Some hospitals and states will put parents in very scary and totally choice-less scenarios. At the same time, there are free-standing birth centers that have holistic, liberal, or new age medical approaches that are very open minded and accepting to the wishes of the parents. There are some hospitals and doctors out there that completely encourage fathers to be present and involved for the entire process.

The underlying fact in all of this is that despite the insistence of both mothers and hospitals, there are no standards for the interaction of women and their birth partners across the board.

What are some of the opinions and stances out there on the role of the father during birth? During my research into different organizations involved that oversee birth scenarios, it became apparent that some establishments feel that there is a standard, and furthermore, they are the ones who set it. Other groups leave the option for the choices of women so open that it borders on the vague and evasive. There are over a dozen groups out there that are associated with childbirth: the American Congress of Obstetricians and Gynecologists, Birthing from Within, the Childbirth and Postpartum Professional Association, International Childbirth Education Association, the list goes on.

This list mostly affects Americans, as it would be too time-consuming to look up all the different groups specific to all the major western countries. Some international groups are used as examples to prove a point. Situations will vary from country to country. Again, the American structure presented here can serve as a model.

The Romans

Perhaps the association that affects the most people in the U.S. is the American Congress of Obstetricians and Gynecologists (ACOG). According to the fact sheet on their website, "Board certification in ob-gyn is a requirement to become an ACOG Fellow, and more than 90% of American board-certified ob-gyns are affiliated with ACOG."[2] One might ask where the other 10% go for their ethics and codes, but it only suffices to say here that one out of ten board-certified OB-GYN's still use other sources for their views and outlooks in respects to labor and birth. These percentages prove there can be splits on the views of standards for men and women during birth, even among licensing associations.

90% of American medical personnel involved in childbirth adhere to one set of standards and ethics. What are the specifics within this code in regards to fathers and other birth partners? On the ACOG website is a pamphlet titled "A Father's Guide to Pregnancy".[3] The section that deals with labor specifically includes this sentence: "Your role during this time is to give your partner emotional support and comfort."

Immediately following that last sentence is this paragraph: "If an emergency occurs during labor or delivery, you may be asked to leave the room. You should leave right away. It is not meant to exclude you. Although there may not be time to explain why at that moment, someone will explain the reasons to you later."

These clips were not taken out of context. It is clear that this association and the hospitals that follow its guidelines believe that a father's role is cheerleading until something serious happens. It is not my purpose to say whether this stance is right or wrong. It does

---

[2] "Fact Sheet", ACOG, accessed December 6, 2013,
http://www.acog.org/~/media/About%20ACOG/ACOGFactSheet.pdf
[3] ACOG, *A Father's Guide to Pregnancy,* accessed December 5, 2013,
http://www.acog.org/~/media/For%20Patients/faq032.pdf?dmc=1&ts=20131205T14262
61146

fall within our scope though to point out that the father does not have the choice of having more active and direct involvement with the birth, if indeed something serious were to happen.

For example, the pamphlet does not address fathers who want to catch the baby, have other children in attendance, or stay during an emergency to be there with his wife regardless of the reason. Later in the pamphlet, other stages of the labor are addressed, such as the ritual of calling friends and family after the birth. Luckily for us, ACOG does offer this little piece of advice near the end of the lecture which illustrates very distinctly the heart of the matter that this book addresses: *"Your old roles are shifting and you need to adapt to new ones."* Does ACOG want the father to adapt to his own views, or their views? It is up to the reader to read the pamphlet in full on their own if they feel that this comment is out of context. Then they can determine if ACOG sets their stances in the spirit of this statement – or against it. It will also prepare birth partners for the true magnitude of some battles that may lie ahead for those who wish to more define their roles.

The Judean People's Front

Just as ACOG sets their own standards for fathers at birth while admitting at the same time that roles are changing – we will look at the views of other groups and associations. It would be impossible to review the positions of all the organizations involved with childbirth. A selection was taken that sufficiently represented large groups and also covered a large number of people.

Another of these groups is the American College of Nurse Midwives (ACNM). This is an organization that certifies and regulates nurse midwives. Here is the stance on fathers and other birth attendants as listed on their website:

"We believe every person has a right to...involvement of a woman's designated family members, to the extent desired, in all health care experiences."[4]

---

[4] "Our Philosophy of Care," ACNM, accessed December 5, 2013. http://www.midwife.org/Our-Philosophy-of-Care

They recognize the desire of women to have other members present at the birth, which we can assume means a sibling, husband, mother, children, etc. It is interesting to note that any type of accommodation beyond that of family members is left completely open. This group does not venture into the discussion or statement of any kind of what the woman may want to happen at her birth, or even who does what. One has to wonder that if the mother wanted her uncle dressed as a clown in attendance – would ACNM allow it? Some may be thankful; however, that at least the option is there if the father wanted to assert his decisions for whatever role he seems comfortable with.

The Popular People's Front of Judea

Birthing from Within (BfW) is a group dedicated to offering education and services to expectant parents, among other options. Their website seems to focus on holistic attitudes concerning the prenatal stage. They do have a class designed for fathers, but I cannot speak to its quality since I have not taken it. However, this group's attitude on the role of fathers can be gleaned from this excerpt on their website:

"In our Special Class for Fathers & Partners, you will learn the secrets to success to be a supportive, compassionate Birth Guardian. In addition, fathers and partners often feel invisible in the birth process. Your Mentor will help you prepare to take care of yourself during labor and postpartum. Much more special resources for fathers and birth partners can be found in our books: **BIRTHING FROM WITHIN** (especially chapters 26-32, 40, 41) and Keepsake Journal (especially Section Four: Birth From the Father's Perspective)."[5]

The first thing that jumps to attention is the focus on the father as a guardian. Where other organizations leave the birth partner's role completely open ended, this group takes a stance, albeit of a very one-dimensional role. They wish to educate others to this same view. We also note no mention of coaching methods in this

---

[5] "What is a Father or Partner to do?" Birthing from Within, accessed December 5, 2013, http://www.birthingfromwithin.com/fathers_partners

description. That is not to say they do not offer it within the class, but it does not make mention of them in the class' details.

The other issues addressed are how to make a father not feel invisible and how to take care of himself during the labor and postpartum periods. This statement implies heavily that the leaders of this organization do not hold fathers who attend birth in very high regard. However, it is safe to say there are differences in their views on birth partners vs. ACOG and ACNM. As for the issue of feeling invisible - this is a concern expressed by many fathers.

The People's Popular Front of Judea

We now come to BirthWorks (BW). This is another education based group that focuses on training other educators and doulas. They seemed to have also developed their own philosophy on how childbirth is to be handled – natural and hands off until outside intervention is needed. This is a crude summary of their policies, but sufficient for our purposes.

In regards to fathers and birth, one of their philosophies is as listed:

"BirthWorks seeks to facilitate a woman's or a couple's personal process in childbearing, and not to impart a preconceived method of labor and birth. Each birth is unique."

Like ACNM, but unlike BfW, the option of having additional people at the birth and what their roles are is left completely open. It is up to the mother to decide who does what and BirthWorks says they will accommodate those viewpoints. Another philosophy down the list makes reference to both parents making decisions in regards to medications and procedures. This implies that the wishes of the birth partner will be honored – which comes close to making a stance, but only in that birth partners are an important part in the decisions made during labor.

The People's Front of Judea

During the research for this chapter, it became obvious that there are many more childbirth education organizations out there than one would think typical. I was expecting two or three, not over a dozen. The fact that fathers aren't aware of this phenomenon may be telling in and of itself. We are getting ahead of ourselves. The largest childbirth education organization out there is the Childbirth and Postpartum Professional Association (CAPPA).[6]

CAPPA trains and educates many different types of positions. For example, they offer certification for different types of doulas and lactation-oriented members, alongside the childbirth education. The language throughout the 'Position on Childbirth' page is heavily directed at the woman and a doula. A quote addressed directly to the father could not be found on that page.

The section on labor support states that a woman should be surrounded by her loved ones in what they call the emotional support team, which includes advocates. These advocates are to help the mother make decisions during labor as they feel she cannot be the sole decider. The fact that they feel a team is necessary in addition to the father seems to indicate a step back from the open ended possibilities discussed by other previous organizations. Yes, the father may be there, but the real work may be left to the three kinds of doulas they offer to educate. Their website doesn't strike me as the best one for accommodating fathers-to-be who wish to carve a new niche.

The Judean People's Front Crack Suicide Squad

The last of the hand-picked organizations we come to is the International Childbirth Education Association (ICEA).[7] This group takes it upon itself to provide support for both birth educators and medical professionals. Where some other organizations focused on natural births or holistic styles – this group explores general alternative approaches. This website is chock full of documents, articles, reviews – many different types of information.

However, on the subject of fathers at birth, or birth attendants in general, information is lacking. In an effort to show fairness, there is a large amount of emphasis on carrying out all of

---

[6] Childbirth and Postpartum Professional Association , accessed December 5, 2013, http://www.cappa.net/
[7] International Childbirth Education Association, accessed December 5, 2013, http://icea.org/

the mothers' choices. We can hope this also means that if she chooses to have an assertive father there, that choice will also be honored. The last paragraph on the mission statement page says that decisions made by family members determines the type of care the mother is to receive. Despite that comment's vagueness, it at least looks promising.

No, I'm Brian!

Of all the organizations selected, not all had views on the role of the father at birth. Of the ones that did venture forth an opinion, ACOG had the most developed stance. Even that stance was narrow and specific, and bordered on the manipulative. In the long view, this proves that for parents who make that first huge step developing their own role – the path will be very long and difficult. Some fathers may feel that the stance described by ACOG is too much even for them. I hope the fathers who may be unwilling to confront the issues raised here will not hold back the rest of us who do.

There will of course be a few who would argue that how do we as fathers even know that women as a whole want us involved in birth – and not just a select random few with the loudest voices? Even though this may be a silly argument, it most likely needs addressed quickly anyway. All I can say to that is even mainstream Hollywood media almost never portrays a woman in the movies who insists that she wants do the whole thing alone.

It is difficult to expand on this point without stacking statistics upon women's birth stories. Needless to say, I challenge any person out there to ask all their female family members with children if they wanted the father around, or at the very least, nearby. On the other hand, books about the increasing need of fathers are starting to become more abundant. These types range from medical explanations to collections of birth stories.

The common sense bottom line is that women want their partners there for the birth. Whether the situation is considered from a strict biological approach, or a broad sociological one – it's inclusive. We're in it, wanted or not, for better or worse. Most fathers don't even know that they can have roles, let alone that they can develop them to their own desires and wishes.

In Chapter One, I discuss the chaos facing fathers in the delivery room. If this chapter shows us anything, it is to describe the chaos. No organization has the same standard or model for the father-to-be to follow. None can even agree that there is chaos, let alone cooperate on solutions. These differing stances hinder the development of roles by ignoring the problem and the need to correct it.

Chapter Three
Historical Aspects

Breathe dear...

All of us have seen a least one movie birth where the woman is on the verge of hyperventilating while screaming in anger at her husband. What a lot of us don't know, which included me up to a few years ago, is that this fast type of breathing was part of a birth method called Lamaze. Luckily, that breathing style isn't included in the Lamaze teachings anymore, as it basically causes the laboring mother to actually hyperventilate. The breathing style has changed to a slower and more relaxed pace. Another thing I didn't know is that there is another model out there, called the Bradley Method, which was published in 1965. Robert Bradley wanted to focus more on involving fathers in the birth – as labor coaches mainly.

There are at least seven or eight different childbirth methods currently out there for fathers to read about, with many more being developed. They run the gauntlet from LeBoyer who says the father shouldn't be in the room, to the previously mentioned Bradley who says the father should be there hand in hand with the mother throughout the entire process. However, what were the opinions and practices of men in the past? What were the views of the ancient Greeks, Romans, and medieval Europeans, among others - about men and the birth process?

Fathers have taken on many different roles in the past. Some were standard and defined by the people of that time. Some were not defined at all, as during the European Dark Ages. It is necessary to examine some examples of the expectations and responsibilities of the fathers at birth throughout some of the key cultures in western history so we can have a better context for examining our own views and stances. The brevity of this chapter is due to the lack of serious research into this field by most historians, and will only allow us to touch on a few specific examples.

The Greek Era

Men in ancient Greece were aware of and comfortable with the existence of midwifery. They spoke of midwives openly, discussed them, and compared birthing to other professions. Socrates spoke of being the son of a midwife, and Plato wrote a book, *Theaetetus*, where Socrates compares his work to that of a midwife. According to Socrates, the midwife delivers children from the wombs of women; whereas he delivers thoughts from the minds of men. We also find another passing reference in the Hippocratic Oath to not using abortifacients.

There is an important fact relating to midwifery in ancient Greece that had a large influence on childbirth. The dissection of cadavers and its subsequent study of anatomy were considered a religious taboo. The only knowledge physicians, surgeons, midwives, and the occasional layman had of anatomy was through the study of dissected animals. For most fathers, the medical process of labor was a complete mystery.

In spite of the lack of the common anatomical knowledge, myths developed around birth and laboring women. Stories of women giving birth through unusual as well as normal circumstances were probably the most important source of information about birth available to men: "Myths are filled with events surrounding birth and death and the special power of women to withstand and control the two crises through which every human being must pass."[8]

Luckily for us, we have some information about how Greek fathers handled these situations. Sources on Greek marriages generally agree that between the ages of thirty and thirty-five was the best time for a man to marry and have children. The years between sixteen and thirty were spent in war and politics. Girls were expected to marry around the ages of 15-17 and start having children immediately.

---

[8] Powell, Barry B. *Classical Myth*. (New Jersey: Pearson Prentice Hall, 2004), 39

Myths and midwifery aside – men didn't simply drop off the planet during their wives' pregnancy. Obviously they had to be there for conception and then to accept the child into the family. It is also safe to assume the he was one of the first to hold and inspect the infant after the birth. However, when the mother did indeed go into labor, the father was nowhere to be seen.

The reasons for the father's absence during labor are very clear. In ancient Greece, there was a concept called miasma, defined as: "1. noxious exhalations from putrescent organic matter; poisonous effluvia or germs polluting the atmosphere; 2. a dangerous, foreboding, or deathlike influence or atmosphere."[9] To the Greek fathers, both birth and death were thought to produce fluids that made the persons, and house, involved to be unclean. There were numerous rituals and methods for purifying a house in which birth or death occurred. Greek men usually chose not to be near either of these circumstances.[10]

In *Daily Life in Greece*, the author describes this situation: "It followed that any birth constituted a defilement not only for the mother, but for the entire household: this was why no accouchement (childbirth) could ever take place inside a sanctuary."[11] In an earlier paragraph it is also stated: "Athenian wives had their children at home, with all the women of the house crowding round to lend a hand."[12] Childbirth was a woman-only affair, and even if a father wanted to be present, he had to undergo extra ritual purification afterward.

I'm Sorry... What?

Many have heard of Oedipus. Some know him through the plays of Sophocles and others through the psychological condition

---

[9] *Dictionary.com*, s.v. "miasma," accessed December 7, 2013, http://dictionary.reference.com/browse/miasma?s=t

[10] Powell, *Classical Myth*, 39: "Childbirth was a moment of personal crisis, because many women died from it, but also of enormous pollution, called miasma, because of the blood and other fluids that attend childbirth. No man would come close to a woman in labor. Women's ability to purify the chamber and the child after birth extended to their care of the dead."

[11] Flaceliere, Robert. *Daily Life in Greece*. (London: Phoenix Publishing, 1965), 79

[12] See note 11 above.

created by Freud called the Oedipus Complex. He was the subject of one of the greatest of the ancient Greek tragedies. This mythological character provides a great example for the discussion of the role of the father in Greek culture.

The play was about a child whose father, Laius, was the king of Thebes. At first the king was unable to have a son. He consulted the oracle at Delphi, which was famous for dispensing wisdom, sometimes in the form of riddles. He asked whether or not he was to have an heir. The oracle replied that he would have a son, but this child would kill him and marry his wife, Jocasta.

When Jocasta had a son, Laius ordered the child's ankles bound together. As a result, he was given the name Oedipus, which meant swollen foot. He gave Oedipus to a servant and commanded the servant to leave the child outside, exposed on a mountain to die by the elements. The servant took pity and instead gave the infant to a shepherd. That shepherd then passed the infant to another shepherd and so on until the child ended up in a neighboring kingdom, Corinth.

In Corinth, Oedipus ended up as the adopted child of its king and queen, Polybus and Merope. Later on in his life, someone revealed to him that he was adopted. He asked his parents if this was true. They denied it, but he didn't believe them. To find the truth behind his upbringing, Oedipus also decided to consult the oracle at Delphi. The oracle only tells him that he is destined to kill his father and marry his mother. Deciding that he is indeed the prince of Corinth, he leaves his perceived homeland to avoid killing Polybus.

Oedipus then travels to Thebes. On the road to his true home he encounters Laius, and they have an argument about the right of way. Oedipus kills this man, not knowing that he is his true father. After killing Laius, Oedipus encounters a Sphinx just outside of Thebes. He is told that if he cannot answer a riddle, he will die. He answers correctly and the Sphinx kills itself out of failure. When he arrives in Thebes, Oedipus is crowned its new king for defeating the Sphinx. He then marries the newly widowed Jocasta, not knowing that she is his mother. There is much more to the tale, but the introduction is fitting enough for our purposes.

The example that this myth provides for us is the act of exposure. Laius orders the infant to be left outside to die. That act, leaving a child outside to its death, would seem like a horrible thing to the people of any western society today. Sadly, this was a somewhat regular occurrence in both ancient Greece and for some time in Rome. The majority of the time, the infant was kept and there was a standard of what to do immediately after the birth.

Day 3...

Publicly the father didn't really step in until the tenth day, when the mother and child were considered purified, and only then it was at a banquet so he could name the child. More importantly though, the father had the first three days to decide if he even wanted to keep the child, as abandoning it out to the elements to die was a legal and accepted practice. Girls were more likely to be exposed than boys, as some dowries were too much for poor and rich families alike.

The Greeks justified this practice by the reasoning that they were not killing or murdering the child if it was left out to the elements. Nature, the weather, and animals, etc – were the ones who actually killed the child, the Greek fathers' hands were clean of blood. There were even methods that midwives and doctors considered legitimate in determining if a child was fit to keep. Bathing the baby in cold water or washing it with pure wine to test its crying fervor were some of the more common methods. Too much or too little crying meant that the baby was sickly or unhealthy. There were differing ways of deciding the infant's health from area to area, but the point is understood.

There were other circumstances surrounding the practice of infant exposure. Not all infants died outside and alone. The myth of Oedipus shows that sometimes the act of exposure was not carried out. In other times, a traveler would find the child and rear it as its own. Occasionally, someone would raise it as a slave or prostitute. Additionally, it was not unheard of for a woman to fake a pregnancy and find an exposed child to raise as her own, thereby fooling her husband. Fathers may also have been aware of the barren wife's behavior, and perhaps even supported it. Such indirect, and direct, knowledge would have made it much easier for fathers to rationalize the abandonment of the newborn.

Like Oedipus, many people have also heard of Helen of Troy, Achilles, Paris, and Hector, etc. The Trojan War was the subject of almost the entire book of the Iliad. There were numerous myths outside of the Iliad that were also concerned with its characters. The Trojan character that relates to our topic is Paris, and it wasn't for his abduction of Helen.

The King of Troy at that time was Priam, and his wife was Hecuba. When Hecuba was pregnant with Paris, she had a dream that she was going to give birth to a flaming torch. They consulted a seer who foretold that this child would be the downfall of the city. The seer also said that the child had to die so that the city could be saved. However, neither Priam nor Hecuba could bring themselves to kill the infant.

Priam gave Paris to his chief shepherd Agelaus and ordered him to kill the child, and then show proof of its death. However, the shepherd also could not kill him. Agelaus did have the option of another social custom: exposure. He left the infant on the side of Mount Ida in the hopes that he would die there. However, instead of being killed by the elements or animals, Paris was suckled by a female bear. Agelaus returned nine days later to find the infant still alive. The shepherd decided to raise Paris and gave Priam a dog's tongue as proof of demise.

In this myth, we find many of the same elements from the story of Oedipus. Both fathers had wanted the child dead due to some type of prophecy. Neither of the stories' parents could go through with the act required of them. Both accounts had shepherds who had difficulty with the killing of the infant and finally, the survival of these characters leads to a tragic ending.

The last example is from a partially surviving drama from the Greek New Comedy playwright Menander. *The Shorn Girl*, or *The Girl with the Hair Cut Short,* was written around 315-310 B.C. It would be recognized easily by western audiences as a comedy of errors, comparable to some modern sitcoms. The mother of the two characters died in childbirth and the father had no money to raise them. He dressed them and left them out to the elements. It is not sure how the children survived, but at the end of the play, the father recognized them since someone had kept the clothing they were wearing when they were exposed. The logistics of the act of exposure in this comedy is not important, but simply that it was nothing extraordinary for a comedy to include in its plot a father that dressed his newborns and left them outside to die.

The purpose of this book is not to discuss the extremely complex social aspects and the many varied conclusions that can be gleaned from these stories. I simply look at the where the fathers were during labor in ancient Greece, and apparently they were not anywhere near it. How do our experiences today, in the 21st century, compare to those of both the mythological people and the real citizens who actually lived during that period of time? Are we not more attached to our infants than the warriors of Sparta or the politicians of Athens?

Wait, what day is it?

After the father decides to keep the child, it is included in the purification rituals already prepared for the house and mother. Five to seven days after the birth, a family festival took place in which purification ceremonies were conducted for all those who were involved physically in the birth. Ten days after the birth was the final ceremony. At this ritual, the child received its name and was accepted into the family officially with food and sacrifices.

It now begs the question of where the father was during this entire two-week period. Was he in the house during the birth? Was he staying with friends during the five-to-seven day period before the house was purified? It can be safely assumed that he came into extended contact with the child before the three days was up in order to decide to keep the child. What about those fathers, the random and helpless farmers and shepherds, who found an infant on the edge of their land? It seems that there were many more circumstances facing the fathers of Greek times than those of Middle Ages or industrial Europe, and possibly even before that, since the myths of Oedipus and Paris go back to the 8th century B.C.E. – long before the Golden Ages of Pericles and Sparta.

Roles revolving around birth were extremely complex, but still somehow standard, for the Greek parents. The mother would have to abide by any decision the father made. It must have been very difficult for her to watch the events unfold after the delivery. Fathers also had some very tough decisions to make. The joint venture of childbirth happened in alternating stages between the mother and father. Everyone in this culture was aware of how things could play out, tragically, normal, or otherwise, and they knew what was expected of them.

The Roman Era

Not all exposed infants who survived were destined for tragic ends. Some went on to do great things. In Roman myth, there is a story of two brothers, Romulus and Remus, who were the sons of Rhea Silva, and the grandsons of King Numitor of Alba Longa. Numitor's brother, Amulius, killed him and his sons to take over the throne. He then forced his niece Rhea to become a vestal virgin so that Numitor would have no heirs.

Rhea did become pregnant, although by who differs according to Roman authors. When the twins were born, Amulius ordered them to be exposed out in the wilderness. However, instead of killing them, an animal saved their lives. A female wolf suckled the twins, who were then discovered and raised by a shepherd. These twins then went on to found the great city of Rome. This story implies that exposure of the infant by the father had not changed by the time of the Romans.

In the writings of the Roman physician Soranus, we find one of our best non-mythological sources for the practices surrounding childbirth in the Roman times. His book *Gynecology* was written to be what we now would consider a textbook. It was for the training and licensing of midwives in the Roman culture. In his book we discover a few important differences from the Greek methods of childbirth and the father's role.

For Ròmans, it was the midwife, and not the father, who administered the tests to determine if the child was fit to keep. The midwife had most, if not all, say in the decision of whether the child was worthy of rearing. Once a decision was made, we can wonder who it was that actually left the infant out in the wilderness. It is not hard to see how this would have put even more distance between the father and what went on in his household surrounding the birth.

According to Soranus, we find that there were two other official midwives in attendance, perhaps as apprentices. I think that holding the laboring woman down was their primary function. Based on the reading, it seems as if the primary midwife actually inserted her hands and pulled the baby out. This would also exclude the other non-medical women family members in attendance from actually participating in the labor.

Sometime during the absorption of the Greek culture into the Roman Empire, the taboo surrounding the dissection of human cadavers was done away with. The anatomy of childbirth was a brand new and intensive field that both male physicians and female midwives took great interest in. That topic was also discussed in detail in Soranus' book.

For the layman father, things did not change much from the Greek to Roman period. The aura of mystery was not totally dispelled. We can conclude that miasma and pollution was still a factor, based on the existence of churching methods in the Middle Ages, which were rituals designed to bless the post-birth mother so that she may enter the church again. Not much changes with the introduction of Christianity and through to the onset of the Middle Ages.

Medieval Times

After the Roman era ended, our next best points of historical reference surface in Europe, in the 1500s, perhaps a thousand years later. One half of the views from this time are religious sources: an Old Testament reference to impurity of women after birth, and the

Christian custom of the churching of women. The other half of the reference, thanks to the printing press, is the release of *The Birth of Mankind*, by Thomas Reynalde. These two historical examples will give us a good indication of the roles and expectations of fathers, albeit still indirectly, of the European Middle Ages.

Looking at the religious example first, with the churching of women, we find a trend that must be a survival of Jewish and Roman customs combined. We know from the previous section that Greek (and most likely Roman) men had to wait for their wives and homes to be purified so they could name their children and move on with life. Accounts show that this was still the case for Christians in the Middle Ages, but seen more as an obligation than a true crisis of pollution.

The Jewish side of the story comes from Leviticus 12:2-7 (King James Version). It states:

"2. Speak unto the children of Israel, saying, If a woman have conceived seed, and born a man child: then she shall be unclean seven days; according to the days of the separation for her infirmity shall she be unclean. 3. And in the eighth day the flesh of his foreskin shall be circumcised. 4. And she shall then continue in the blood of her purifying three and thirty days; she shall touch no hallowed thing, nor come into the sanctuary, until the days of her purifying be fulfilled. 5. But if she bear a maid child, then she shall be unclean two weeks, as in her separation: and she shall continue in the blood of her purifying threescore and six days. 6. And when the days of her purifying are fulfilled, for a son, or for a daughter, she shall bring a lamb of the first year for a burnt offering, and a young pigeon, or a turtledove, for a sin offering, unto the door of the tabernacle of the congregation, unto the priest. 7. Who shall offer it before the LORD, and make an atonement for her; and she shall be cleansed from the issue of her blood. This is the law for her that hath born a male or a female."

It can be assumed that the father or another male family member supplied the animal offerings discussed in the quoted paragraph. While this may not be news for a lot of Jews or

Christians, we must look at in the context of where the father was supposed to be or what he was expected to be doing during this period. We can also say that this type of thinking can be retroactively applied to the period leading up to the European Middle Ages.

What is not seen in this point in history is reference to the house being unclean, thus differing from the Greek version, and perhaps relating more to the Roman account. There is also no account of if and when the father may keep or name the child. For these fathers then - house and social rituals and naming are most likely just matter-of-fact circumstances that are handled on the side during the mother's separation from normal conduct. In essence, fathers had to deal with the impurity of birth and the purification of the mother, and not much else.

There may have been another function of the churching, although we may never know when this function appeared. The indirect medical reason, of becoming sexually active again, as pointed out by author Lucy Worsley:

"Lying-in continued until the conclusive ceremony of 'churching' a month after the birth, when the woman left the house to return to church (and came home to return to her husband's bed)."[13]

Where's my pope hat?

Since this is in the King James Version of the Old Testament, it is natural for a Christian equivalent to have formed. The Christian side of the story is from the Catholic Encyclopedia under the entry of 'churching of women':

"A blessing given by the Church to mothers after recovery from childbirth. Only a Catholic woman, who has given birth to a child in legitimate wedlock, provided she has not allowed the child to be baptized outside the Catholic Church, is entitled to it. It is not a precept, but a pious and praiseworthy custom (Rituale Romanum), dating from the early Christian ages,

---

[13] Worsley, Lucy. *If Walls Could Talk, An Intimate Portrait of the Home,* (New York: Walker and Company, 2011), 20.

for a mother to present herself in the Church as soon as she is able to leave her house (St. Charles Borromeo, First Council of Milan), to render thanks to God for her happy delivery, and to obtain by means of the priestly blessing the graces necessary to bring up her child in a Christian manner. The prayers indicate that this blessing is intended solely for the benefit of the mother, and hence it is not necessary that she should bring the child with her; nevertheless, in many places the pious and edifying custom prevails of specially dedicating the child to God."[14]

There is no stark reference to impurity in this passage, but I believe it still heavily implied socially. It can be inferred at this point in history that custom is more important than actual spiritual cleanliness, but it is not removed altogether. The father having an unclean or impure mother in his house seems to have been the norm in Europe from Greek times to the Middle Ages. In common with the case of the Jewish impurity, there is no mention of the house being unclean. In both cases, there is also no reference at all to the practice of infant exposure. We can safely say that this practice seems to have died out with the fall of Rome.

Is there a printing press on the Internet?

The other point of reference for the 1500s, *The Birth of Mankind*, is more direct in its views toward fathers and childbirth. I must say here that technically this book had many different authors and publishers prior to Reynalde's version. For the sake of brevity, we will simply refer to its last incarnation. This book is of the same importance of Soranus' *Gynecology* and indeed much of the former's content is directly from the latter.

Both Soranus and Reynalde were male physicians skilled in anatomy. They were primarily concerned with the licensing of midwives, as they make very apparent in their writing style and target audience. Both authors deal with the strict medical view of the birth, and do not discuss the purification or cleanliness issues.

---

[14] "Churching of Women," New Advent, accessed December 5, 2013, http://www.newadvent.org/cathen/03761a.htm.

This area of childbirth obviously fell within the realm of the local priest, as previously discussed.

The first thing that jumps out in *The Birth of Mankind*, and gives a good indication of the father's whereabouts during birth, is this quote: "Also the midwife must instruct and comfort the party (individual), not only refreshing her with good meat and drink, but also with sweet words, giving her good hope of a speedful deliverance."[15] There are no instructions for other birth attendants. There are always historical assumptions and quotes about birth being a woman-only affair, but having a direct instruction such as this proves the father's absence during birth, for any and all reasons.

Where Soranus does not deal with naming rituals and other family affairs after the birth, Reynalde does offer some advice and social musings. In his introduction, Reynalde makes a fervent plea that laymen (husbands, who are not physicians) should also read his book:

"It shall be no displeasure to any honest and loving woman that her husband should read such things; for many men there be of so gentle and loving nature toward their wives that they will be more diligent and careful to read or seek out anything that should do their wives good, being in that case, than the women themselves."[16]

His writing style implies that he may be arguing against the social norms, and, based on the previous historical accounts, isn't hard to see why. His strongest argument is that if birth was truly an unnatural process and an unclean offense to society, then doctors and physicians would hate their wives and find them disgusting:

"And if the knowledge of such things which commonly be called the woman's privities should diminish the hearty love and estimation of a woman in the mind of man, then by this reason, physicians' and surgeons' wives should greatly be abhorred and misbeloved of their husbands. And I myself likewise which writeth this book should marvelously above many other abhor or

[15] Reynalde, Thomas. *The Birth of Mankind: Otherwise Named the Woman's Book.* ed. Elaine Hobby. (1560; repr., Surrey: Ashgate Publishing Limited, 2009), 107
[16] Reynalde, *The Birth of Mankind*, 20

loathe women. But to be short, there is no such thing, neither any cause thereto why."[17]

These two passages were written in 1560, the language is a bit different than how we talk today in England or America. Taken into its total account, Reynalde's introduction and pleas to men and women to let the father be more involved in the childbirth indicate that any man who was not a physician or midwife had no idea whatsoever of what went on during birth. How long it took, what the woman felt, its stages, possibilities, medical warning signs and positive markers – all these factors were unknown to and outside the realm of the father.

There was obviously some gray area. Fathers in the European Middle Ages knew that a stork didn't drop their newborn down the chimney. They most likely heard snippets of particular information from women throughout their life. In regards to the process as a whole, knowledge of what was happening, let alone how to participate in any useful way at all – fathers in this culture were simply removed from the entire circumstance. Unlike the Greek and Roman fathers, these men had access to the information that dispelled the mystery.

I did find another interesting point of reference also from about the same time as Reynalde's writings. In her book *Men and Maternity*, Rosemary Mander briefly mentions the 16th century practice of "nidgeting". Apparently when a man's wife began her lying in, it was his job to go out to all of her friends' houses, knock on their doors, and announce that they were needed for the birth. There is no mention of where the father went after that, although we can assume that it wasn't back to the house where his wife was laboring. Perhaps he went down to the bar to celebrate the impending birth, as we will soon see from a 17th century novel. This would also explain Reynalde's plea for all fathers to be more involved, if they were down at the taverns drinking.

---

[17] Reynalde, *The Birth of Mankind*, 20

The Enlightenment Period

Our next example comes from a novel written in 1751, titled *Amelia*. The context of the excerpt is that two military men are traveling, and they meet. One has his sister with him, the other his wife, and both women are pregnant. Both the sister and the wife gave birth relatively close together in time. What follows is an account of one of the men being confronted by a midwife during the birth, and another account of the two men meeting during the other birth.

I tried to maintain all of the original spelling but left out the unusual word capitalization. I also included the editor's footnotes in the excerpt. It is dangerous to make too many assumptions on one fictional entry, but I believe that this is a very important piece of literature that accurately reflects public opinions. Even if taken at face value, this is an interesting read and offers at least the opinions of one man from the 1740s.

"In this company we passed two or three months very agreeably till the Major and I both betook ourselves to our several nurseries; my wife being brought to bed of a girl, and Miss Bath confined to her chamber by a Surfeit, which had like to have occasioned her Death (fever or fits, often caused by diet, which could indeed be fatal).

"Here Miss Mathews burst into a loud laugh, of which when Booth asked the reason, she said she could not forbear at the thoughts of two such nurses: and did you really, says she, make your wife's caudle yourself? (A thin gruel, mixed with wine or ale, sweetened, spiced and warmed, given for health reasons to women who had just given birth.)

"Indeed, madam, said he, I did, and do you think that so extraordinary?

"Indeed I do, answered she, I thought the best husbands had looked on their wives lying in as a time of festival and jollity. What did you not even get drunk in the time of your wife's delivery? Tell me honestly how you employ'd yourself at this time.

"Why then honestly, replied he, and in defiance of your laughter, I lay behind her bolster, and supported her in my arms, and upon my soul, I believe I felt more pain in my mind than she underwent in her body. And now answer me as honestly: do you really think it a proper time of mirth, when the creature one loves to distraction is undergoing the most racking torments, as well as in the most imminent danger? And - I need not express any more tender circumstances.

"I hand to answer honestly, cry'd she. - yes, and sincerely, cries Booth. - why then honestly and sincerely, says she, may I never see heaven, if I don't think you an angel of a man.

"Nay, madam, answered Booth - but, indeed, you do me too much honour, there are many such husbands - nay, have we not an example of like tenderness in the Major? Tho' as to him, I believe, I shall make you laugh. While my wife lay in, Miss Bath being extremely ill, I went one day to the door of her apartment, to enquire after her health, as well as for the Major, whom I had not seen during a whole week. I knocked softly at the door, and being bid open it, I found the Major in his sister's antechamber warming her posset (hot milk curdled with alcohol and flavored with sugar, herbs, and spices, believed to have medicinal effects). His dress was certainly whimsical enough, having on a woman's bed-gown, and a very dirty flannel nightcap, which being added to a very odd person (for he is a very aukward thin man near 7 feet high) might have formed, in the opinion of most men, a very proper object of laughter. The Major started from his seat at my entring into the room, and with much emotion, and a great oath, cry'd out, is it you sir? I then enquired after his and his sisters health. He answer'd, that his sister was better, and he was very well, Tho I did not expect, sir, cry'd he, with not a little confusion, to be seen by you in this situation. I told him, I thought it impossible he could appear in a situation more becoming his character. You do not? Answer'd he. By god I'm very much obliged to you for that opinion; but I believe, sir, however my weakness may prevail on me to descend from it, no man can be more conscious of his own dignity than myself. His sister then called to him from the inner room; upon which he rang the bell for her servant, and then after a stride or two across the room, he said with an elated aspect, I would not have you think, Mr. Booth, because you have caught me in this Dishabille (careless or informal dress, from the French 'deshabiller,' to undress,) by coming upon me a little too abruptly, I can't help saying, a little too abruptly, that I am my sisters nurse. I know better what is due to the dignity of a man, and I have shewn it in a line of battle. I think I have made a figure there, Mr. Booth, and becoming my character; by god - I ought not to be despised too much, if my nature is not totally without its weaknesses. He utter'd this, and some more of the same kind, with great majesty, or is he call'd it, dignity. Indeed, he used to some hard words that I did not understand; for all his words are not to be found in a dictionary. Upon the whole, I could not easily refrain from laughter; however, I conquered myself, and soon after retired from him, astonished that it was possible for a man to possess true goodness, and be, at the same time, ashamed of it."[18]

We can draw many conclusions from this excerpt. First according to the midwife, it probably was unusual for fathers to be at the birth. However, from the defensive attitude of Mr. Booth, it seems that men who were not at their births were not true men, even if they were battle hardened. True men could care for their brothers in the heat of battle, but also their sisters and wives in the throes of labor.

For me it is obvious, that like today, the issue was just as divided then as it is now. Some men were not at their children's births, other men considered it their paternal duty. However, there were men who wanted to be there because they loved their wives, or in this case, his sister. It should also be noted that they were useful, and not just in the room pacing nervously.

After the book Amelia, opinions started to change. Lucy Worsley, in her excellent book *If Walls Could Talk, an Intimate Portrait of the Home*, has revealed more on this area of study of how

<hr>

[18] Fielding, Henry, *Amelia*, ed. Linda Bree. (Andrew Miller, 1751; Ontario: Broadview Press, 2010), 153-154

birth was viewed from the father's perspective during this time period.

"Babies made their first appearance amid a world of women, with males being kept out of the birthing chamber until deep into the eighteenth century. 'My wife's mother came to me with tears in her eyes,' wrote Nicholas Gilman in 1740. 'O, says she, I don't know how it will fare with your poor wife, hinting withal her extreme danger.' Mr. Gilman was entirely in the hands of his mother-in-law for information about the life or death of his spouse, and childbirth was the one part of household life over which men had no control."[19]

This account seems to contrast with the situation given in the Amelia novel. We can only wonder if these are two opposite ends of the extreme, or if the fictional story was wishful thinking on account of the author. It is definitely food for thought. Regardless of which was the true social standard, more changes were on the way. Here are some good examples of stances that eventually survived into our modern era.

"The squeamish attitude of the nineteenth century introduced a novel reluctance to talk about pregnancy. As early as 1791, a writer in *The Gentleman's Magazine* noticed a growing trend for references to pregnancy to be seen as errors of good taste. 'Our mothers and grandmothers, used in course of time to become with child,' he wrote, but 'no female, above the degree of chambermaid or laundress, has been with child these ten years past...nor is she ever brought to bed, or delivered.' The genteel lady should merely inform 'her friends that at a certain time she will be confined.' The downside of all this tasteful gentility was that women began to think of pregnancy as an illness, and Victorian books about childbirth began to refer to it among 'the diseases of women.' In the bedchamber, as in society at large, women began to be seen as fragile, vulnerable and incompetent at looking after themselves."[20]

---

[19] Worsley, *If Walls Could Talk, An Intimate Portrait of the Home*, 20
[20] Worsley, *If Walls Could Talk, An Intimate Portrait of the Home*, 26

"Alongside the idea that pregnancy was an illness, the lying-in hospital began to grow in popularity. Slowly childbirth was taken out of the bedroom, out of the home altogether, and into the public realm."[21]

The Victorian Era

Our next step in history takes us to Victorian England, specifically John Tosh's *A Man's Place: Masculinity and the Middle Class Home in Victorian England*. We must also take this moment to point out that books mentioning the matters of fathers and childbirth in historical periods are few and far between, therefore the finding of this book was a welcomed turn of good luck.

Having said that, this book was well researched and excellently written. John Tosh breaks the norm of assuming that fathers had no impact, indirectly or otherwise. He realizes that this topic is worth researching and writing about. If only more authors took his stance and challenged the assumption that there wasn't enough evidence or that it wasn't worth the effort.

There is no way to summarize the role of the father in Victorian England better than Tosh himself, here are his conclusions:

"What did change in the early part of the nineteenth century was men's relation to childbirth itself. Medical lore dating back to Aristotle attributed the key role in reproduction to the potency and agency of the male: he was the progenitor of life, while the female was the passive carrier. The Christian notion of God, the Father greatly reinforced this way of thinking. Social practice in Early Modern society reflected the same message. Before and after the birth, the mother was rigidly secluded; the father was the central figure in the social drama of childbirth, celebrating with family and friends, arranging the baptism and hiring a wet-nurse. He was confirming his manhood as well as performing his patriarchal duties. From the late eighteenth century, however, scientific enquiry began to place more emphasis on conception as a natural process which unfolded

---

[21] Worsley, *If Walls Could Talk, An Intimate Portrait of the Home,* 27

within the woman's body, with ovum rather than the seminal fluid holding key to the mystery of generation. Childbirth came to be seen as the fulfillment of a woman's femininity, rather than a disruption to her performance of the duties of wife. This was one reason why the prestige of motherhood was on the increase, and it meant that the mother as the bearer of the child became the central figure, rather than the father as bearer of the family name. Instead of being the master of ceremonies and focus of public attention, the father was on the way to becoming the nervous bystander of recent times.

"Paradoxically, however, he was now more often found in the delivery room. Traditionally, the seclusion of the mother-to-be had to be extended to her husband, who was not present during birth – though he was likely to be the first person to enter the room after the happy event. By the 1840s, it had become commonplace for husbands to be in attendance for the birth itself..."[22]

Much information can be gleaned from this excerpt and applied both retroactively to past outlooks, and forward to the evolution of the modern stance. First, there is no mention of church purity standards. It may have passed from simple custom to mostly obsolete church practices. Second, we see a reference to more fathers now being in the delivery room with the mother. I even discovered that Charles Darwin administered chloroform to his wife during labor![23]

In his summary, Tosh notes changes that had significant impact upon fathers and their views and subsequent interaction with childbirth. The ancient tradition of the father removing himself entirely until it was safe to hold the child and oversee the family affairs was being challenged due to a number of factors. Such factors were changing social views on the woman's role in birth, the downplaying of the father's biological importance, and the removing of the religious aspects after the birth. The roles that had endured

[22] Tosh, John, *A Man's Place: Masculinity and the Middle-Class Home in Victorian England*, (New Haven: Yale University Press, 1999), 80-82
[23] Worsley, *If Walls Could Talk, An Intimate Portrait of the Home*, 25

from Greek, Roman, and Jewish times were challenged, revised, or discarded.

From the late 18th to the early 20th century, there was only one real change in the way childbirth was handled that directly affected the father. The majority of births moved from the home to the hospital.[24] Some fathers may have considered it a stroke of luck that the mess of childbirth was now a problem for someone else. Others might have felt robbed of that unique and exciting event. In any event, many historians concerned with the evolution of pregnancy refer to this as the Hospitalization Phase.

Modern Times

From the 1900s to the 1960s, the hospitalization phase kicked in, and also kicked the fathers out of the delivery room. A good example of this type of thinking is presented in *The Social Context of Birth* in Tim Blackshaw's chapter "Fathers and Childbirth":

"It therefore came to be regarded as normal and appropriate professional practice to exclude fathers, and subsequently this was integrated into both lay and professional health beliefs and behaviours, albeit with regional variations. The 1959 British Medical Association (BMA) publication *You and Your Baby* is a good example of public exposure to medical beliefs about fathers and the birth:

"The last requirement of all for a successful delivery at home is the husband - the poor father. If he is of the right mentality, and very few are, he may sustain his wife's morale during the first part of her labour. Otherwise he is best employed making tea, keeping the kettles boiling, and answering the front doorbell. (Kitzinger, 1987: 150)"[25]

---

[24] Goer, Henci, *The Thinking Woman's Guide to a Better Birth*, (New York: Perigree, 1999), 202: "In the 1920s in the United States, middle-class women began having babies in hospitals with physician attendants. By the mid-1920s, half of urban births took place there, and by 1939, half of all women and three-quarters of urban women gave birth in hospitals."
[25] Caroline Squire, ed., *The Social Context of Birth*, (Oxford: Radcliffe Publishing, 2009), 223

By the 1970s, both mothers and fathers had fought and won the battle to reinstate the father's place in the delivery room. However, by that time, a new profession had arisen which is unique in our examination of the father's place during birth. I believe this new concept shines a giant spotlight on the issue at hand, even though that wasn't the true purpose of the idea. Most fathers today have heard of a doula. This is a newly defined profession, for up until now many fathers did not know about the methods of midwives and wet-nurses, let alone other birth attendants. Here is the first definition of a doula.

"Dana Raphael first popularized the term *doula*, a Greek word meaning woman caregiver, in her 1973 book, *The Tender Gift*. She used it to describe women who provided help and support to women after childbirth."[26]

There is a very fine line being walked with the discussion of this profession. It is not my purpose here to belittle or cast this term in any negative light whatsoever. Having said that, it can now be mused as to whether this profession was created subconsciously to fill in the gap by an absent father who may or may not provide a supportive environment for the mother. It might not be a coincidence that this role was officially recognized during the same time that Bradley and other medical professionals tried to get fathers more involved in the birth process. Goer also mentions in her book, that there is a clear distinction between the duties of a father and doula, that the latter does not replace the former. One still may wonder.

Uh, where am I?

With all standards and consensus gone, many people have tried to fill in the gap of what the father is supposed to do during birth. Some parents have even moved beyond the home vs. hospital choice. What I call third-party locations have been introduced; i.e. birthing centers and off-the-path scenic locales, among many other unusual places. I even watched an online video documenting a

---

[26] Goer, *The Thinking Woman's Guide to a Better Birth*, 178

woman having an unassisted birth in a tropical lagoon far removed from cities and hospitals.

Up until the Victorian times in England, and perhaps until the American 1920s, there were some varying standards. Fathers could choose to be in attendance and also had the option of determining his role in relation to the birth. He could be the master of ceremonies. He could ensure the proper hiring of medical associates. In some cultures, the father could ensure proper purification rites were held. He could be a support partner or a mere witness.

Now that all those roles have been replaced or rendered obsolete, modern day fathers find themselves unprepared and unable to face many new types of situations – almost as many as the ancient Greeks (albeit with far less tragic consequences.) The difference from the past is that there is no tradition or pool of knowledge to draw from. When the gauntlet of possibilities is thrown wide - the fathers are left behind wondering if they can determine their own roles alongside the mothers. It will be a great historical loss to future generations who might wish to look back at our own time and find nothing to research or write about.

My hope was to present a linear timeline of specific examples of the father's activities around birth within a strictly Western cultural perspective. If the father was either there or not it is useful to try to understand why. Perhaps to gain a better perspective, context, and understanding of what fathers want in today's world.

Chapter Four
Barriers and Solutions

Why can't we do that?

When all standards and practices from the past, whether good or bad, are gone – it seems that new problems and criticisms arrive, or are created. Any effort that a father may put forth to re-establish his involvement during childbirth is likely to be met with scorn, derision, or just simple indifference from all corners of life. However, history has shown us that any group with the desire and determination can fight and change the status quo.

Our biggest challenges must be recognized so that they can be overcome. The previous chapters proved that fathers' roles have been done away with. By extension, the barriers in this chapter are in contrast to men re-establishing their own power to affect their roles, let alone to recreate those stances. While some of the issues to be discussed may be obvious to some, taken altogether and over time – they can wear down anyone's resolve.

It is not the purpose of this chapter to paint a bleak picture and discourage the would-be birth partner from wanting to develop their own stance in regards to childbirth. Fear not, for every problem there is an answer. For fathers wishing to re-establish their roles at childbirth, there are solutions presented to the barriers discussed. There exists an arsenal of options available. Some are common sense; others may take some skillful subtlety. The bottom line is that the resources are everywhere for fathers to take the initiative.

Do women speak English?

Women have to decide how they want their birth to go before the father can determine his place in it. To take a step back, fathers-to-be must make sure they know exactly what their wives want. There can be no assumptions about what the wife wants when it comes to the location, OB, stance on drugs, or attendants, along with the many other variables in regards to her birth. Communication is of the utmost importance. Not communicating about the upcoming birth is probably one of the most important barriers to address.

A mother is not on sure footing herself at times. If she has to re-explain things to her partner or they just don't get it no matter how many times it is explained, it will put the mother in a very tough spot. She may not react well and will handle the ups and down of birth in a less than 100 percent frame of mind. The same goes for your stance, as the birth partner. There can be no room for doubt in the mother's mind as to where you stand and your views on matters when she is completely focused on laboring. She will need to know that you will remember her wishes. On the flip side, it is important to remember that she will *never* be totally incapacitated.

Even though the most important solution to best overcome all other barriers, as well as this one, is communication between the mother and father, this doesn't have to mean couples therapy, touchy-feely evening sit-downs over dinner, or long walks in the park. They don't have to write a dissertation on what they expect or what they want their stance to be. If the partners start discussing right away, at or before pregnancy, nine months is plenty of time for most parents. Extremely unusual circumstances may take more lengthy chats, obviously.

The answer to this barrier is simple. Assume nothing. Take nothing for granted. Yes, the father will have to sit down and hammer out the smallest details with the mother before he can decide on his role. This is not an impossible task. Couples make complicated decisions all the time such as buying a car, moving to other cities, etc. It is not unusual for couples to discuss the details of birth in the same manner they would as if they were buying a house.

Good ole Uncle Bob...

One of the most complex situations facing a father is the reaction and inclusion of other family members during the birth. These run the gauntlet from benign and indifferent to horrifying and legally atrocious. Even if a mother were to choose a by-the-book hospital birth, there are always instances where a family member decides that they may know better than the prospective parents. Other family members often try to make decisions for the parents. This situation can be a spiky barrier for many fathers.

There may also be some family expectations, traditions, and standards that a daughter or prospective mother wish to break away from. Some fathers may not feel it necessary to adhere to the tradition of the infants getting the father's last name. Some parents may decide not to circumcise. Other parents may choose not to vaccinate. These are just a few examples of decisions that have to be made. They are hard enough in and of themselves, let alone with family members opposing them.

No matter what type of birth decisions are made, there is usually an outspoken family member who wishes to impose their will on the situation. Normally, this would be a mere nuisance, but with so many other uncertainties facing the parents in today's chaotic birthing world, it is not conducive at all for when the father decides on a stance for himself. It is also worth noting that a hostile family member may not have had much chance to oppose birth choices in the past, (like Victorian England,) when roles were much more standard.

There is a short supply of research on family interference and judgment that doesn't require delving into statistics and birth stories. Therefore, an analogy will have to do. In the movie *National Lampoon's Christmas Vacation*, there was a man named Clark W. Griswold who tried wrangle his family into a Christmas at his house. It turned into a hilarious nightmare. Even though it was unrealistic Hollywood humor, it still is relevant to my point. He was working with a tradition that had very established rules, roles, events, and conduct.

Imagine that you are tasked with creating a new holiday. This holiday has to be created from scratch and also has to be slightly controversial. You cannot use any other holiday as a model. This event must take place at a location of your choosing. The flak that you would get from all sides, from all family members, would be awe-inspiring, like watching a natural disaster. This is the position in which mothers and fathers unknowingly find themselves in today's society in regards to childbirth. Basically, sometimes a family can be accepting of other members who wish to do a home or third-party location birth. Other times, they are an obstacle who will threaten to call social services if the mother isn't strapped to a table and gutted by the nearest local medical intern.

The first solution to the family as a barrier is holding fast to decisions agreed upon. If the mother and father are a united front as to the chosen roles they will fulfill during the upcoming birth – the family resistance will be less severe. The first obvious thing a family will notice is that it is much harder to criticize two people than it is one. A mother without the support of the father, and vice versa, makes a much better target for intrusive relatives.

Another solution is keeping low-profile and talking with vagueness. There are many birth stories out there about how the parents just nodded and smiled every time a family member asked about the details of the impending birth. The mother and father just waited and told the family what happened afterward. Answers such as 'we haven't picked a hospital yet,' or 'we haven't found a doctor we like yet,' can work very well. One has to be careful as this approach can also backfire and make the parents look like they need decisions to be made for them.

My favorite approach to fend off intrusive family members is what I called the Bullcrap Method. Luckily for the parents who may wish to use this tactic, most relatives out there don't do any of their own personal research. All the parent has to do is get on the Internet, or use a birth book, and memorize a few statistics. When confronted by an intrusive family member – just rattle off a few of the statistics and tell them because of these numbers, you have come to some vague conclusion. Bombard any naysayer with an overflow of numbers and information. More often than not, this will suffice in throwing the family member off the track. If the parent does indeed have a relative in the medical field, then it is best to not use this method unless you plan to back your bluff up with real numbers and conclusions.

Hospitals have locker rooms?

There are obviously prospective fathers and mothers out there who are doctors, obstetricians, or work in other childbirth-related fields. Another difficult barrier facing parents is when decisions concerning their upcoming birth contradict the hospital policies where they work. Examples are home births, non-vaccination philosophies, anti-epidural stances, etc. While the roles of the mother and father aren't as standard as those per se in the Roman Era and Middle Ages, hospitals and some medical associations have their own ideas about how the way things should go for the parents during labor.

I am not a medical professional of any sort, so only speculation and other personal narratives can be offered. It is a given that hospitals expect most births to happen in their buildings. It is also easy to offend the strict policies of many of the medical organizations that run hospitals. For example, there may be some women who are married to doctors or other such medical personnel (or are themselves doctors or OBs) – but still want an unassisted home birth. In possibly more rare cases, there may be doctor's wives (or women doctors) who want to have a third party location birth, with no drugs, and no vaccines.

These scenarios can put the medical career parent in a very rough position. On the one hand, they would most likely want their position and choices respected. On the other hand, they may face serious criticism and ostracism from their peers and superiors at work. There are some solutions available to the medical career parent in this unique situation. One is very private and discreet birth. However, some laws and states make this very difficult.

Another solution is early dialogue with the appropriate medical superiors. Some hospitals may be supportive of any decisions if approached early on in a mature and prepared manner. In this case, all the parent has to do is stay open and honest with his coworkers and peers. Perhaps coworkers can be told that another hospital was chosen so that some privacy may be kept and some extra stress avoided.

This situation is addressed in Leah Hazard's *The Fathers Home Birth Handbook*. One of the couples dealt with are both nurses and decided to have a home birth with twins. They had difficulty convincing their coworkers and family that a good and sound decision was being made. In the end the parents discovered that the more they stuck to their guns and remained steadfast, the more coworkers took them seriously. Conviction may be the best solution for this type of situation.

Oh crap, it's the cops!

There are many possible places for a mother to choose to have birth. Unfortunately, some states have passed laws that enforce, to varying degrees, the requirement that all births must take place in hospitals. Some states allow parents and midwives to have non-hospital births – but have set the restrictions extremely high. Ask any midwife about getting politicians or government officials to affect any kind of change in hospital policy, and you will have wished you brought a lunch for the rest of the conversation. Some states have also mandated what types of drugs must be given to the infant, such as vaccines and silver nitrate.

The bottom line is that the laws can vary greatly from state to state in regards to any and all types of birth situations and decisions. The legality of many birth decisions is a subtle, but very important barrier for many parents. For those who wish to have an out of hospital birth, it may seem like they may have to hire a lawyer to find out what they can and cannot do. Luckily for those unknowing parents, sometimes the home-birth midwives who practice in that state are very well acquainted with the local laws.

There are couples out there who have managed to have home and third party locale births in states where it is illegal in every sense of the word. It can be done. A convenient truth is that if the mother accidentally had a child before she had time to get to a hospital, there is nothing the government can do about it. Am I instructing you, the reader, to lie to your government or break any laws? No. However, accidents do happen.

For those who live in states where laws are strict, there are some options available. It is not uncommon for some couples to rent a hotel (or birth center) across state lines and have a birth there. It is always helpful to become familiar with as many of the local laws as one can before making decisions about where and how the birth takes place. If time is a factor, there are usually political action groups or midwives who are very familiar with the laws of the land that the parents live in.

Some mothers and fathers are lucky and find that the laws don't contradict to their specific desires. In these cases, the hospital may have done all the legal legwork and the couple needs to spend no time dwelling on the legality of their choices. In many other cases, however, the parents may find themselves fighting against both the hospital and the state for the type of birth they desire.

There is an inverse relationship between how much legal navigating a person must do for a home or third party locale birth versus having a standard hospital birth. The former requires much more than the latter. It is up to the parents to decide how far outside the norm they wish to go for their ideal birth. If there is any doubt about decisions concerning specifics about a planned birth - the best solution is to always check with online advocacy groups.

What's a murse?

Traditionally, hospitals' stances go hand in hand with the local laws. Some states may leave legislation lax and let the hospitals determine the norm. It is rare to find a both a state and a local hospital that is mostly hands-off during childbirth. The methods of navigating the intricacies of hospital rules are most often the same as winding through the ways that the state thinks childbirths should go.

Hospitals, medical associations, and OBs operate independently from the government, but they do try to influence each other. Not all hospitals and OBs are worthy of being demonized, but this chapter focuses on barriers – and they certainly fall into that category many times. A lot of hospital policies are designed to remove as much power from the mother as possible, and don't recognize any from the father at all. There are also some facilities who are hands off unless the mother requests intervention. The reality is that there all shades of gray in between these two stances.

One of the hardest things facing fathers in tense scenarios is defending their wife's choice against the hospital's stance. Many hospitals view the laboring woman as totally incapacitated as soon as her water breaks and feel little need for consent for any type of procedure whatsoever. There are some doctors who want to give the mother drugs the second she breaks into a sweat. Some OB's will try to schedule a C-Section in the third month of pregnancy, before any details about the fetus is known.

We must not forget that almost all hospitals are places of business, not centers for philanthropy. Many OBs will also be very quick to turn the mother into a neat and clean statistic with a cookie-cutter birth plan. Chances are the mother may not agree with these birth plans either. These plans may include anything from drugs and surgery to uncomfortable laboring or birthing positions and possibly risky inductions. OBs and hospitals may frustrate the wife, in which you are the main support. Some may not let children or other family members attend the birth. Many hospitals will not support parents who wish to not vaccinate or opt out of circumcision.

The father must be prepared to be bullied if the mother's choice goes against their policy, or if the hospital does not get the consent they want for risky procedures they want to perform. Such bullying tactics include, but are not limited to: scare tactics involving worst case death scenarios, lengthy legal procedures, transferring to another hospital, or the calling of social services. Threats of all kinds have been documented to have been used by hospitals to enforce their policies.

In some cases, hospitals and their related medical associations go out of their way to lobby the government for laws to support their views, sometimes regardless of current research, or at times, in reaction to it; this still causes confusion, as no two medical associations or hospitals have the same views. This also confuses legal standards, which can vary greatly from state to state, especially for those parents who want non-hospital or medically-attended births such as third party locales or unassisted homebirths.

Arming yourself with as much information as you can with regards as to where you live, either by your own research or with the help of the local midwife community, coupled with online advocacy groups, will help you fend off any resistance that may come your way. Once you feel confident about your choices, have a birth plan set in stone, and have researched many of the local and state laws concerning your birth choices; it is very easy to stand your ground against aggressive hospitals and social groups. At the very least, the parents can shop around different hospitals, birthing centers, and perhaps even measure the distance to the nearest state line. When parents reach that place where they can operate comfortably with hospitals and state laws, then the father may truly flex his wings and develop his role for the birth.

I thought blood was red?!

Many men are not comfortable with the sight of blood. It's a whole new world when it comes to the numerous other bodily fluids that are involved with childbirth. Recognizing the stages of labor while coming into contact with the bodily fluids represents a significant challenge for people in general, let alone the fact that fathers are not prepared for the physicality of childbirth. Oddly enough, this situation is one of the first things men think of when childbirth is mentioned. The image of a laboring woman covered in a rainbow of fluids is a very common barrier for fathers. Some may even go so far as to decide to not want to be a part of the birth, let alone develop a role for it.

The physicality of childbirth offers some of the funniest solutions. Ultimately, there is no clear way to prepare for the fluids a father will come into contact with during the birth. This solution also assumes that a home or third party local birth was chosen, as this problem is not really dealt with by the parents who have a hospital birth (other than perhaps just seeing lots of blood). Probably the closest analogy I can come up with as a solution is the dressing of an animal for its meat, i.e. the skinning, the gutting, and then the trimming. It may sound very vulgar, but in reality, humans have mostly the same bodily fluids as other mammals except skunks and other oddities. If a father has no problem working hands-on in this type of situation, then childbirth should be a breeze.

For fathers who have never experienced the dressing of an animal in any way, shape, or form, it is a bit trickier. Perhaps it would be a good time to call that hunter friend if the mother decides to not have a hospital birth. Maybe a father could intern at a butcher shop for a week or two. From personal experience, relying on internet videos doesn't come close to the real thing.

It takes how long?

There is no dancing around it. For the majority of history, with a few windows here and there, fathers were not involved in the childbirth process. It is new ground. Finding oneself in new territory is difficult enough. Add the slightest chance of the loss of life to two individuals (the infant and the mother) and that mix is a monumental responsibility. Without sounding New Age-y, finding the determination to put oneself into this type of circumstance is not an everyday matter for most fathers out there. Not all of us are used to making quick and life-impacting decisions in intense situations. This is the barrier of personal resolve.

Even if one does make that first step of mustering up the personal resolve, it may not last for the entire labor. Some births can take a long time. Hopelessness and despair can affect both the mother and father during a long and difficult birth, no matter the location. This is also one of the hardest things for which a father must prepare. The birth partner may think of the labor as a race that could be a sprint, or a marathon. They may also view labor as a testing session for school; the test may be short multiple choice, or a very long essay exam.

The awkwardness and feeling like an alien around the laboring mother is also related to the barrier of personal resolve, and pretty much instinctive in many respects. This feeling can become ten times stronger for births that take place at a hospital. It is my opinion that this is one of the least understood, yet one of the most important, factors that needs to be addressed by both parents. This feeling may also involve the wife, as she also may be making the father feel out of place, if even unknowingly, at the subconscious level. I think the best solution to this circumstance borders on the philosophical. The birth partner must be firm in the belief that they are indeed helping, and not just there as a witness.

No amount of preparation can ready the father for all the possibilities and variables that may happen during a long birth, or even one of the short and easy ones. A father committed to the birth may come to the conclusion halfway through that he is not prepared, and uncertainty may start to slip in, even momentarily at times, in all birth scenarios. This can have extremely detrimental effects on the mother if she senses it.

Finding the personal resolve to endure what sometimes is a two day affair with no sleep, and other times a three hour joyous and uncomplicated event, is no easy task. It is akin to a really long drive for a family vacation. It can be long and arduous, or it can be pleasant. Either way, a parent knows that hundreds of things can go wrong, or everything can go right. The same outlook must be applied to childbirth, at any location.

It may sound obvious, but there are many fathers out there who incorrectly assume that since there were no complications during the pregnancy, there will also be no complications during the actual birth, or vice versa. Murphy's Law loves to rear its ugly head at births. The best approach is simple: walk that fine line of prepare for anything, but don't have a nervous breakdown doing it. For people who run marathons, have EMT training, are firefighters, etc., attending a birth is more of an ordinary day-to-day event. For the rest of us, it takes a lot of mental preparation.

Do I need a pre-med degree for this?

It is hard for me to admit this, but some awareness of the medical aspects of labor is a necessity. Mothers who decide that they want a non-hospital birth are notorious for buying and reading dozens of books filled with medical terminology relating to the birth process. A father has two obvious choices: read all the same books or don't.

In some situations, this reading binge by the mother is part of a preparation stage, but in most cases, this knowledge is a must. The fear of making mistakes or not knowing what is going on due to not knowing all the medical terminology is a common theme for most fathers. The only way to offer a solution here is to state that it is up to the father to decide when he has absorbed enough information to feel comfortable being involved in a birth.

What's Pitocin?

A decision was made to treat the barrier of fear and scare tactics separately. I mentioned this briefly in the hospitals section, but I can elaborate here. These methods are also used by family members, government officials, hospitals, friends; people from all areas of society. Horror stories, urban legends, and old wives tales will pressure the mother and father relentlessly every time a discussion about the birth comes up, even for cookie-cutter hospital births. Why people feel the need to discuss these things with soon-to-be parents will probably never be fully explained.

Even the best father out there, a U.S. Navy Seal who is iron under pressure anywhere and anytime, can get blindsided. OBs and hospitals have been known to assert themselves as an authority over the parents so that they can use fear and scare tactics on mothers whose views differ from that hospital's policy. Both parents can be in 100% agreement on every little thing that they want to happen before the child is born. In many cases, the mother has to deal with the extra stress of the father fighting off intrusive hospital staff. Any attempt to stick to a chosen role or birth plan may simply fall apart at times like these.

For those births that are to take place in a hospital, it is best to research what the specific stances and rules are at the particular establishment. To take those stances for granted and just choose the nearest hospital may not be a wise decision. If you live in the city, or even for the people who live far out in the country – there is almost always more than one hospital to choose from. As we discussed previously, hospitals can differ greatly in how they treat the parents during childbirth. Take the opportunity to choose which facility may be best suited to the needs of the mother and father.

It is not uncommon for C-section focused hospitals, who wish to keep their budgets balanced, to tell a father that the wife and baby will die if she isn't sliced open in the next five minutes. The majority of these threats are usually bogus, and the hospitals will argue to their dying breath that their assumption was right. For the father, preparation and knowledge is the best solution. Both men and women are loathe to read about statistics concerning C-sections, but sometimes it must be done, especially if you get an OB who shoves the mother into a cookie cutter diagnosis.

We can't forget urban legends from friends and family. What if something bad happens at home during labor? What ifs can be applied to any situation and are some of the most common scare tactics used. Driving a car, water skiing, and hiking – all these scenarios can be talked about in the what-if context for hours. That doesn't stop most people from doing them anyway. The same attitude is applied to birth. For example, some relatives insist that you will need drugs to experience more of the birth. They will say: "The pain will be so much that the mother won't remember much. No one should have to experience that much pain." These assumptions are very biased and extremely subjective; dismissing them as such when told is usually the best solution.

Viruses and bacteria are different things?

The most developed and most easily dispelled barrier is what I call the Layman's Catch 22. One part of this dilemma is the assumption that certain men, i.e., surgeons, doctors, OBs, etc., know everything about birth, but many times choose to be far removed from it, even when it's their own wife.

The other premise of the Layman's Catch 22 is that birth is a mystery to non-medical oriented men. This is obviously false. All men today know that the stork doesn't bring children, or that women don't go into a room and come back out with a baby like they just came out of the kitchen with a pot roast. In Roman times, Soranus wrote extensively and with many minute details about all aspects of birth and even post-birth medical situations. Soranus and all other men of his day, and even before with Socrates and his Theaetetus, knew how labor went. Many men in the past considered themselves in charge of the licensing of midwives. In their books, Reynalde had almost the exact same tone as Soranus; men should be masters of anatomy and midwives should be monitored. Childbirth may have had an aura of mystery in Ancient Greece, but with the addition of Roman surgery, there wasn't much mystery left.

Medical practitioners know many of the specifics about birth, and laymen know many of the general processes about birth. Why many men still treat pregnancy and labor as if it were some form of ancient mystical alien technology from a bad documentary confuses me. Don't get me wrong, there is still a lot of spirituality and life affirmation surrounding birth. However, pregnancy and birth should be respected by fathers in today's era, not feared, as in very ancient times. Once a father realizes this critical understanding, then choosing how he wants to be involved in the birth will be very easy.

Are we having a baby or passing a bill through Congress?

Due to these barriers, fathers today basically cannot develop roles. For any mother who wants her significant other involved, it is chaos. It is like watching a wife ask her husband to play a complex card game that he has never heard of. OBs and hospitals are notorious for being hostile to any choices that deviate from the 9-5 birth. These circumstances now force the father to make his own way from scratch in every sense of the word. The father of today has the difficult fate of awaiting his wife's decision of how she wants the birth to go, how he personally wants to be a part of it, and finally, to what extent both of the parents' desires are possible in their current state, society, family, etc.

There are going to be dozens of people, clueless midwives, nurses, doctors, family members, co-workers, etc., who will try to tell you and your wife what to do. This chapter is to help the father realize that there are only two options. One is throw your wife to the wolves and let her fend for herself, or remain by her and encourage, defend, support, and stand up for her. There really isn't much middle ground. It's all in or nothing. The father may find himself confronted by police or social services, or by a cadre of angry family members. It could go the other way though, with church members, family, or others who form a defensive wall around the mother, against people who make it their business to make women birth the way they want, not the way the mother wants to. There are many horror stories out there about very bad OBs and midwives. Part of the responsibility of the father lies in preparing for any scenario that involves these types of people. There are crackpots and fruits in any field, and medicine is no different.

Ultimately, it is up to the parents which of these solutions to use and to the varying degrees they are used with the other possibilities. When used properly and together, the parents will avoid most confrontations and have a rock solid basis of how they will handle the birth and have their decisions respected. Due to changing history and the conflicts of all parties involved in childbirth, a huge gap has formed between the best and easiest birth scenario to the worst and hardest type. The would-be father must think about all these possible scenarios and options: from barriers and hard deliveries to solutions and easy births. Anything can happen on the road to birth. The active father has many road bumps to navigate so that he can define his role more easily.

Chapter Five
Postpartum Disorders
and Birth Trauma

How do veterans react to traumatic births?

I discovered that getting fathers to talk about birth in general is difficult. It turns out that I was originally and incorrectly only looking at the transmission of useful knowledge and positive experiences. Many of the women I spoke to about what happens during labor brought up the point that there were fathers out there who were dealing with very traumatic experiences or some form of depression after the birth. This made sense and I felt at fault as a researcher for not considering this sooner. There are birth stories out there by fathers who talk about bad experiences, even traumatic ones – but they were never categorized on their own, they were just thrown in with the rest of the birth stories: good, bad, and uneventful.

In light of this new understanding, I want to discuss definitions and resources for parents about understanding postpartum depression (PPD) and birth trauma (BT). I think that there will be three positive outcomes. The first is that fathers can be better prepared for anything negative that may happen during or after the birth. The second outcome would be fathers discussing and helping future fathers with their own experiences. The third outcome would be that fathers could better help the mothers, as well as themselves, in the treatment of these conditions.

It should be clear now that I am not speaking about fathers who have negative reactions to normal or uncomplicated births due to unpreparedness, or other such factors. For example, birth trauma can include birth complications that affect the health or development of the infant, inhumane treatment by medical professionals, or loss of life (mother, baby, or both). These are very extreme examples and can be extremely rare. This puts me in the very difficult position of talking about these conditions, but yet not stooping to fear-mongering. How can expectant parents truly prepare for, or prevent traumatic births, and how can they deal with the possible depression after childbirth?

It is true that how parents handle the prevention, recognition, and treatments may vary from person to person based on unique personality types. However, the treatment, support groups, and counselors all operate the same, regardless of the birth partner's personality type. It is also impossible to say whether or not one type of personality will recognize any of these conditions sooner than another. Basically, the methods for the prevention, recognition, and treatment are universal to all parents. Even though I promised to go easy on the medical terminology earlier on, I believe that an exception can be made for this particular topic.

There is a distinct separation in the existences of PPD and BT. The medical view is that postpartum disorders are conditions that result from hormone changes in both the mother and father after birth. Birth Trauma is either - an event, a condition, or both; the result of something extremely traumatic or life threatening happening to either the mother or child during the birth. Some of the different definitions can be very complex. I hope this chapter will make the issues clearer.

The many views and definitions out there currently are very chaotic, sometimes even contradictory. These conditions occupy the fringes of the birthing experience. In fact, some of the definitions are so elusive, that my wife and I got into an argument about the best way to define combat scenarios, shell shock, trauma, PTSD, birth trauma, and the possible combinations and overlap between all those terms. There is very little in print about its relationship with women during and after birth, and even less in regards to fathers. There is some decent material on the Internet about it, and it is possible to find websites that go into these concepts in much more detail than this chapter, but my goal here is for preparation and prevention more than diagnosis and developing better definitions.

I will try to consolidate all the best definitions and resources for parents who wish to understand these conditions. Fortunately, this information can be applied retroactively for parents who have witnessed or participated in traumatic births in the past but are unsure of what to make of it, as well as parents who experienced some form of postpartum depression.

When dictionaries fall short

A major obstacle in the quest for finding the best definitions for postpartum disorders and birth trauma is that some medical stances differ from the layman's view, if included at all. Most medical stances focus strictly on the physical and psychological. For example, the welfare of the *infant's* physical and mental state immediately after the birth is what is defined when it comes to birth trauma. Unfortunately for parents, in most medical definitions there is no real consideration of the mother or father as well, physically or mentally. The two medical sources I used were *Taber's Cyclopedic Medical Dictionary* and *Stedman's Medical Dictionary*. They had all the definitions I needed, except neither had any entries about Postpartum Post Traumatic Stress Disorder, that I could find anyway.

And the categories are...

The first section will deal with the conditions that are categorized as postpartum disorders. Even though Baby Blues is a legitimate after-effect of many births, my main focus is on Postpartum Depression (PPD) a.k.a. Postnatal Depression (PND), and Postpartum Psychosis (PPP). Both Taber's and Stedman's have entries for Postpartum Blues and Postpartum Psychosis. Only Taber's has an entry PPD/PND. I only included the definition, symptoms, and treatments. I did not include the diagnosis part of Taber's entry on PPD because it was mostly about medical tests that most laymen could not perform.

Here is a good overview of Postpartum Psychiatric Disorders:

"During the postpartum period, about 85% of women experience some type of mood disturbance. For most the symptoms are mild and short-lived; however, 10 to 15% of women develop more significant symptoms of depression or anxiety. Postpartum psychiatric illness is typically divided into three categories: (1) postpartum blues (2) postpartum depression and (3) postpartum psychosis. It may be useful to conceptualize these disorders as existing along a continuum, where postpartum blues is the mildest and postpartum psychosis the most severe form of postpartum psychiatric illness."[27]

Baby Blues

Taber's: "Postpartum Blues: A period of heightened maternal emotions that follow the birth of a baby, typically beginning in the first three to five days after childbirth. Common symptoms are irritability, emotional lability, and tearfulness, although exaggerated happiness may also be reported. Unlike postpartum depression (a persistent mood disturbance after childbearing), postpartum blues typically resolves in a week to ten days."[28]

Stedman's: "Postpartum Blues: Mood disturbance (including insomnia, weepiness, depression, anxiety, and irritability) experienced by up to 50% of women the first week postpartum; apparently precipitated by progesterone withdrawal."[29]

Postpartum Depression

Taber's: "Postpartum Depression. Depression occurring up to 6 months after childbirth and not resolving in 1 or 2 weeks. The disease occurs in about 10% to 20% of women who have recently delivered.

"SYMPTOMS: Affected mothers typically report insomnia or hypersomnia, psychomotor agitation or retardation, changes in appetite, tearfulness, despondency, feelings of hopelessness,

---

[27] "Postpartum Psychiatric Disorders," Massachusettes General Hospital, accessed December 5, 2013, http://www.womensmentalhealth.org/specialty-clinics/postpartum-psychiatric-disorders/

[28] *Taber's Cyclopedic Medical Dictionary*, 21st ed., s.v. "postpartum blues"

[29] *Stedman's Medical Dictionary*, 7th ed., s.v. "postpartum blues"

worthlessness, or guilt, decreased concentration, suicidal ideation, inadequacy, inability to cope with infant care needs, mood swings, irritability, fatigue, and loss of normal interests or pleasure.

"TREATMENT: Drugs, (e.g. tricyclic antidepressants and serotonin reuptake inhibitors), counseling, or electroconvulsive therapy are all effective therapies. PPD support groups are generally helpful to women. Online support networks include Postpartum Support International (www.postpartum.net) and Depression After Delivery (www.charityadvantage.com/depressionafterdelivery/home/asp.) Carefully designed studies have shown that nursing care aids in the diagnosis, prevention, and treatment of this disorder."[30]

Postpartum Psychosis

Taber's: "Postpartum Psychosis: A psychosis that develops during the 6 months following childbirth, the highest incidence being in the third to sixth day after delivery through the first month postpartum. The symptoms and signs include hallucinations, delusions, preoccupation with death, self-mutilation, infanticide, distorted reality, and interpersonal dependency. Therapies used to treat this condition include estrogens, electroconvulsive therapies, lithium, and neuroleptic drugs."[31]

Stedman's: "Postpartum Psychosis: An acute mental disorder with depression in the mother following childbirth."[32]

Hormones, especially progesterone, almost certainly play a part, but these medical texts do not include any social considerations. Basically, how much time and effort a mother has to recover after a delivery may determine the length and severity of postpartum disorders. This is a time when the level of involvement of fathers and their roles is extremely important.

The next section deals with conditions that are reactions to negative experiences not necessarily caused by hormonal changes or differing levels of support and recovery during the first week after

---

[30] *Taber's Cyclopedic Medical Dictionary*, 21st ed., s.v. "postpartum depression"
[31] *Taber's Cyclopedic Medical Dictionary*, 21st ed., s.v. "postpartum psychosis"
[32] *Stedman's Medical Dictionary*, 7th ed., s.v. "postpartum psychosis"

62

birth. These are Post Traumatic Stress Disorder (PTSD), Postpartum (or Postnatal) Post Traumatic Stress Disorder (PP-PTSD), Basic Trauma, and Birth Trauma. Neither Taber's nor Stedman's had entries on PP-PTSD, or non-medical birth trauma. Let's start with the basics, PTSD and trauma.

Post-Traumatic Stress Disorder

Taber's: "Post Traumatic Stress Disorder: Intense psychological distress, marked by horrifying memories, recurring fears, and feelings of helplessness that develop after a psychologically traumatic event, such as the experience of combat, criminal assault, life-threatening accidents, natural disasters, or rape. The symptoms of PTSD may include re-experiencing the traumatic event (a phenomenon called "flashback"); avoiding stimuli associated with the trauma; memory disturbances; psychological or social withdrawal; or increased aggressiveness, irritability, insomnia, startle responses, and vigilance. The symptoms may last for years after the event, but often can be managed with supportive psychotherapy or medications such as antidepressants."[33]

Stedman's: "Post Traumatic Stress Disorder: Anxiety disorder that is a syndrome of responses to extremely disturbing, often life-threatening, events such as combat, natural disaster, torture, maltreatment, or rape."[34]

Trauma

Taber's: "Trauma: 1. A physical injury or wound caused by external force or violence... 2. An emotional or psychological shock that may produce disordered feelings or behavior."[35]

Stedman's: "Trauma: An injury, physical or mental."[36]

Outside of childbirth, these are legitimate medical circumstances. Neither definition is strict in the sense that PTSD can only happen in certain events. Conventional wisdom dictates, and

---

[33] *Taber's Cyclopedic Medical Dictionary*, 21st ed., s.v. "post traumatic stress disorder"
[34] *Stedman's Medical Dictionary*, 7th ed., s.v. "post traumatic stress disorder"
[35] *Taber's Cyclopedic Medical Dictionary*, 21st ed., s.v. "trauma"
[36] *Stedman's Medical Dictionary*, 7th ed., s.v. "trauma"

these medical entries agree with, that PTSD can result from a variety of situations. The next reasonable step then would be to apply this condition to the realm of childbirth. This is where Postpartum Post Traumatic Stress Disorder and what I call Layman's Birth Trauma comes in. Since neither of my medical texts had any entries on this concept, I used a state health agency and Wikipedia, (yes, I admit to using this website) for basic definitions.

Postpartum Post Traumatic Stress Disorder

"Postpartum PTSD was first described in 1978. Since then, over 60 studies have been published. After excessively painful labors, those with a disturbing loss of control, fear of stillbirth or complications requiring emergency Caesarean section, some mothers suffer nightmares and intrusive images and memories (flashbacks), similar to those occurring after other harrowing experiences. They can last for months. Some avoid further pregnancy (secondary tocophobia), and those who become pregnant again may experience a return of symptoms, especially in the last trimester. Rates up to 5.9% of deliveries have been reported. There is some evidence that early counseling reduces these symptoms. Enduring symptoms require specific psychological treatment."[37]

"Approximately one to six percent of women experience Postpartum Post-Traumatic Stress Disorder (PTSD). Most often, it is caused by real or perceived trauma during childbirth, such as unplanned C-section, health issues with the baby, and feelings of powerlessness, poor communication and/or lack of support and reassurance during the delivery. Women who have experienced a previous trauma, such as rape or sexual abuse, are at higher risk for experiencing postpartum PTSD."[38]

[37] "Psychiatric disorders of childbirth," *Wikipedia*, last modified September 24, 2013, http://en.wikipedia.org/wiki/Psychiatric_disorders_of_childbirth

[38] "Postpartum Post-Traumatic Stress Disorder," State of New Jersey, Department of Health, last modified July 12, 2012, http://www.nj.gov/health/fhs/postpartumdepression/ptsd.shtml

Our last term, Birth Trauma (BT), is where things get even more confusing, since BT can be a condition, a cause, and an event. It is then defined even further as either medical, psychological, or both. It can be described physically and medically for the baby such as physical complications, and also considered a psychological event for the baby, a theory developed by Otto Rank. Even beyond the medical aspects, it is a condition affecting the parents who witnessed or experienced a traumatic birth. Lastly, it can also be the event that caused the Postpartum PTSD. Here are the medical definitions:

Medical Birth Trauma

Taber's: "Birth Trauma: 1. Injury to the fetus during the birthing process. 2. Otto Rank's term to describe what he considered the basic source of anxiety in human beings, the birth process. The importance of this concept is controversial."[39]

Stedman's: "Birth Trauma: 1. Physical injury to an infant during its delivery. 2. The supposed emotional injury, inflicted by events incident to birth, on an infant which allegedly appears in symbolic form in patients with mental illness."[40]

Non-medical or Layman's Birth Trauma

"When we talk of birth trauma, we mean Post Traumatic Stress Disorder (PTSD) that occurs after childbirth. We also include those women who may not meet the clinical criteria for PTSD but who have some of the symptoms of the disorder.

"PTSD is the term for a set of normal reactions to a traumatic, scary or bad experience. It is a disorder that can occur following the experience or witnessing of life-threatening events. We usually recognize these as things like military combat, natural disasters, terrorist incidents, serious accidents, or violent personal assaults like rape. However, a traumatic experience can be any experience involving the threat of death or serious injury to an individual or another person close to them (e.g. their baby,)

---

[39] *Taber's Cyclopedic Medical Dictionary*, 21st ed., s.v. "birth trauma"
[40] *Stedman's Medical Dictionary*, 7th ed., s.v. "birth trauma"

so it is now understood that Post Traumatic Stress Disorder can be a consequence of a traumatic birth."[41]

"Post-Traumatic Stress Disorder is an anxiety disorder that can develop after exposure to a terrifying event or ordeal where grave harm occurred or was threatened (i.e.: to the women and/or her baby). PTSD is one of the most serious effects of trauma. We are familiar with PTSD in torture victims, combat soldiers, sexual assault victims and war survivors, but PTSD after childbirth has a long history of dismissal. Current estimates of the number of women who develop all symptoms of PTSD after childbirth are about 6-7%. Far more women develop some of the symptoms of PTSD. All of these women suffer birth trauma."[42]

For some odd reason neither medical text discusses the causes of these conditions, with the exception of the medical aspect of birth trauma to the infant itself. Statistics are all over the place about the percentage of women who get these conditions, who is more predisposed, how long either parent suffer from them, etc. The only consensus is that Postpartum Psychosis is much rarer than PPD. A quick review reminds us that of the two types of conditions, PPD and BT, the former is caused by hormonal changes and the level of postpartum support, the latter is caused by a traumatic event during labor.

Postpartum PTSD and Birth Trauma are defined in the same way by four different sources. Some people would imply that a traumatic event at birth causes the postpartum PTSD. However, I would offer that birth trauma is a better developed term in that it includes the event that caused the psychological condition, as well as a description of the condition. Regardless of the overlap and differences, both of these terms describe real situations.

[41] "What is Birth Trauma?" Birth Trauma Association, accessed December 5, 2013, http://www.birthtraumaassociation.org.uk/what_is_trauma.htm
[42] "Post Traumatic Stress Disorder," Birth Trauma Canada, accessed December 5, 2013, http://birthtraumacanada.org/2.html

The core issue is that whatever causes these conditions happens at birth or immediately after. All these definitions are well and good, but this is about the birthing hour – why are these factors important? Heavy emphasis must be on the causes, with prevention as the key. Knowledge of, prevention, recognition, and treatment falls within any role that the father or birth partner chooses. My goal is to make the father aware of what may happen, and to help parents who experienced any of these conditions to seek out proper treatment. My conclusion is that BT is the event, PP-PTSD is the condition.

It also seems possible that parents could suffer from both sets of conditions: PPD and BT. There are resources on the Internet for treatment if necessary. I think that the best solutions are preventative measures from information and choices, coupled with preparation.

In essence, for postpartum disorders, lack of care is the cause, and more care is the cure. The care could be from just the birth partner, or a large circle of family and friends. My favorite approach for planning and the prevention for PPB, or PPD, after birth is based on Sheila Kitzinger's theory of birth as a psychosexual experience. Her idea is that birth is much more than a biological or physiological event. It is an active, social, and passionate experience. Not to downplay PPD; but to me that implies that the prevention and also the treatment of PPD could be compared to serious cuddling after serious sex.

The mother may be worn out physically, but postpartum cuddling could mean many things. It could mean showing sincere forms of affection after the experience. It could be giving her space and taking care of day to day logistics while also helping with her physical and mental recovery. This psychological form of cuddling after an intense psychosexual encounter might help the father get his bearings back as well.

Possible ways to prevent birth trauma are a bit trickier. Medical birth trauma falls more within the realm of medical variables, and there is no way of predicting accidents or bad judgment calls by medical staff. As for the Layman's Birth Trauma, based on the definitions, the best measures would be to make sure that the laboring mother feels in control of her own body and the birthing experience, is totally aware and informed of all that is happening during labor, regardless of location, and that she has the right to make whatever choices she wishes to make. I realize that this sounds much easier than it looks, but we have to start somewhere. The definitions provided should give the parents a good source of information on how to recognize if either parent is suffering from these conditions. Counseling is usually the most recommended form of treatment. At the end of the chapter is a list of resources for the treatments of all the conditions discussed herein.

I originally pondered how expectant parents could possibly prepare or prevent PPD or Birth Trauma; and how could they deal with the depression and postpartum PTSD after childbirth, especially Postpartum Psychosis. I believe that social planning, preparation, and care will prevent or treat the postpartum disorders. I also believe that the best hope of preventing Layman's Birth Trauma is a well thought out birth plan that is taken very seriously by hospital staff, or serious preparation for home or third-party locale births. Lastly, for Postpartum Psychosis, I think that birth partners can do what they can to not make it worse, but its causes are most likely some form of a severe chemical imbalance prior to the childbirth, and there isn't much that they can do about it, other than seek professional help. It might also be helpful to consider, (or research), whether the mother may be at risk for PPP for future pregnancies.

Any role that a birth partner chooses should include time for preparation and planning in the beginning for the lessening of the effects of postpartum disorders. Time for follow-through and execution of those plans after labor should also be included. A Birth Plan should be a primary focus in the early part of the pregnancy for decreasing the chances of Medical Birth Trauma. For births not in a hospital, Layman's Birth Trauma is not as serious a consideration, but chances can still be decreased by information and preparation.

68

Support Links, Articles and Books:

Birth Trauma Association,
http://www.birthtraumaassociation.org.uk/

Birth Trauma Canada, http://birthtraumacanada.org/

Solace for Mothers, http://www.solaceformothers.org/

Babbel, Susanne, PhD, MFT. "Partpartum PTSD Versus Postpartum
Depression", http://www.psychologytoday.com/blog/somatic-
psychology/201012/postpartum-ptsd-versus-postpartum-
depression-0

Birth Without Fear, Mr. "Emergency C-Sections, Incubators, &
Hospital Protocol: Men Experience Birth Trauma, Too",
http://birthwithoutfearblog.com/2011/08/28/emergency-c-
sections-incubators-hospital-protocol-men-experience-birth-
trauma-too/

Campbell, Denis. "Too scared to push: big rise reported in birth
trauma",
http://www.guardian.co.uk/lifeandstyle/2010/nov/14/scared-
birth-trauma-midwives

Dewar, Gwen. "Childbirth trauma and post traumatic stress: What's
wrong with the status quo?"
http://www.parentingscience.com/childbirth-trauma.html

Stone, Katherine. "20 Things I NEVER Want to Hear or Read Again,
Postpartum Depression Edition",
http://postpartumprogress.com/20-things-i-never-want-hear-
again-postpartum-depression-edition

Chapter Six
Fathers and Birth in Movies

Citizen Who?

The issue will never be settled as to whether art reflects life, or if life reflects art. I believe that it is both. Sometimes people imitate the artwork that inspires them. At other times, artists depict what they see around them in their work. There is also a lot of gray area in between those two points of understanding. Movies certainly lie in the nether region of influence between those two points. For our discussion, I will not say which end of the spectrum Hollywood movies are closest to, art or life. I will say that those movies are meant to entertain, and are often watched by millions of people. I discuss the movies seriously, even though they are obviously just for entertainment. As shown in the art vs. life example, fathers are either influenced by these movies, or the true life actions of men are the source of inspiration for these movies. Neither conclusion is acceptable for fathers wishing to assert themselves in the delivery room.

This chapter focuses on the roles of fathers portrayed in movies. What we see in movies does affect our opinions, and vice versa. Not many people argue with the truth that movies affect popular culture. *He who has not judged people seen in movies, is the same as he who has not watched one.* It must be stated here that I am not a film critic. I don't care if these movies are social commentaries, rom-coms (romantic comedies,) or anything else, category-wise. Most film critics would probably see that my summaries are around the high school level. My point here is not to review the movies in and of themselves. People take away different things from all movies. I am evaluating these movies for extremely specific circumstances. The brief portrayal or attendance of fathers and any expectations of them up to and during the birth, is the focus of this chapter.

In addition to movies, there are hundreds of regular TV shows that have birth scenes of their own. It would take a ridiculous amount of time to go through them all and watch their labor scenes. And even if I did, there is no way to avoid being accused of cherry-picking the ones that backed up my opinions. I also believe that what is seen in TV shows reflects similar views that we see in the movies. For these reasons, I will not discuss birth scenes on TV shows.

Regarding fathers in movies, we must ask certain questions:

- How are fathers at birth portrayed in the movies?
- Are these portrayals accurate? Or do they project stereotypes?
- What are fathers up against in terms of stereotypes, images, expectations, etc?
- What are the effects of the characters we see in the movies?

Six movies were chosen based on a number of factors. I chose a timeline since we started seeing more pregnancy movies, beginning in the 1980s. Movies from then to today are also the most relevant to the present-age fathers and grandfathers. It had to be a high grossing movie to show that a lot of people saw it and therefore, that it had some effect on pop culture. It is also important to discuss somewhat realistic pregnancies, so that *Rosemary's Baby* and other such movies were ruled out. Also, I did not watch them in the order of when they were released.

In my opinion, these are the six best representative movies about pregnancies and birth that show fathers or some kind of male attendant. I am not saying that female or other types of birth partners don't exist, just that it is really hard to find that circumstance in movies. The three areas focused on in each movie were the fathers' actions, the mothers' expectations, and the reactions of family, friends, and medical staff (social realm). Notes on the movies will almost be shorthand, as the conclusion is the more important part. I will not be discussing the movie's entire plot, only what is relevant to our focus.

1988 – *She's Having a Baby*
1995 – *Nine Months*
1995 – *Father of the Bride, Part II*

2000 – *Where the Heart Is*
2007 – *Juno*
2007 – *Knocked Up*

Knocked Up: Ben as the father, Alison as the mother.

Father's Actions

 During pregnancy: Ben is a slacker stoner before the pregnancy, and he has the initial denial of circumstance and responsibility when he finds out. He is accepting and encouraging of her decision to keep the baby, and asks what he should do, admitting he is clueless. They both buy what books are available at the mainstream bookstore. Ben doesn't read the books at first, as he thinks the books are worthless. He argues that ancient Egyptians didn't have them in the past. He exhibits the usual movie fear of change or being changed. Ben has a short dialogue with his father who just says to read the books and nothing else.

 During labor/birth: Ben does panic occasionally. He is anxious, but calm when told to be. Eventually, Ben does read the books prior to labor and shows knowledge of stages and other medical information. He does the talking for the mother and fights for her choices. Ben stays by the mother's side when he can, massaging her back. When the controlling sister tries to send him out of the delivery room, he in fact sends her outside. He stays behind her during pushing stage. Ben holds the baby while Alison recovers and sleeps after the delivery. Most importantly, Ben does not allow arguments in the room with the mother by taking all confrontations outside.

Mother's Expectations

 During pregnancy: Alison has initial uncertainty after the positive pregnancy tests. She wants to keep romance in their sex life during the pregnancy, as well as commitment. Alison goes through many obstetricians to choose one she wants, and is very picky about it. She wants support and empathy on all matters between her and Ben. She does not want to not be alone throughout pregnancy, and wants the same doctor throughout the entire thing. Alison wants Ben to read the birthing books that they bought together. She places lots of emphasis on the books. There is no talk of breastfeeding in whole movie.

During labor/birth: Alison wants to stay relaxed. She wants a natural birth (no drugs), and to follow her birth plan closely.

Social Reactions

During pregnancy: There is another couple with kids in the movie, Alison's sister and her husband. They set a bad example by always fighting and maintaining an unhappy marriage. Every doctor the main characters see always assumes they are married. There is the total gauntlet of all ranges of reactions from their entire social circle. There is no help or advice on the actual labor from anyone, in any sense. Alison's boss wants to avoid talking about the gross stuff when he finds out.

During labor/birth: Alison's original obstetrician didn't set aside time to see her at the due date, so she had to accept a new doctor. This new doctor uses scary medical terms to get what he wants, then accuses Alison of being a control freak. Alison's sister doesn't think Ben is mature or important enough to be with Alison in the delivery room, but then respects Ben after he sends her packing.

Summary

Knocked Up sets a good role model after the father's initial transformation. It shows an accurate range of reactions to both the stages of pregnancy and to the labor from the entire social circle of the parents. There isn't much dialogue in terms of real or actual advice between Ben and his father or anyone else. There is a lot of emphasis on the birthing books, in multiple scenes. The movie stresses the importance of transformation for the dad, as in most other pregnancy movies. This transformation is one that changes him from a child in denial, the stereotype, to a mature person ready for parenthood. The mother in this movie didn't have to go through much of a transformation to become ready for parenthood.

Luckily, this is not a movie that shows the father as remaining clueless, even after his acceptance and transformation. His actions at the birthing scene are shown in a positive light. He was calm and made sure to keep the mother calm during labor. He was not shown to be a bumbling clueless idiot as other pregnancy movies show. He knew what was going on. Overall, I thought this movie did not portray a negative stereotype of a father at birth, and was even encouraging for fathers.

Nine Months: Samuel as the father, Rebecca as the mother.

Father's Actions
During pregnancy: Sam has the typical initial denial about the pregnancy. He refuses to change his lifestyle to the point where Rebecca leaves him. He has to watch the ultrasound for the reality to kick in. He takes a Lamaze class on his own. He convinces Rebecca to take him back after he proves his readiness by abandoning his old lifestyle choices.
During labor/birth: Samuel goes into panic when labor starts. There is a comedy of errors on the way to the hospital. When there, he blunders around the delivery room and almost hurts Rebecca by letting go of the wheelchair she is in. He does not remain calm and passes out at the sight of a large needle. The doctor also passes out while saying that is why women handle the birth; men can't handle needles and blood. He gets into a fist fight with the other dad by breaking his camera. They are in the same room with another laboring woman due to not enough space in the hospital. Samuel is of no real help, not even as a coach or support person. He does not stay next to her for much of the labor. The other dad in the delivery room is supportive at first, excited but calm, before the fist fight occurs over the broken camera.

Mother's Expectations
During pregnancy: Rebecca is a passive character. She is uncertain at times about what she wants. She wants Sam to marry

her, but doesn't tell him. She wants support on all levels. There is no talk of breastfeeding in whole movie.

During labor/birth: Rebecca wants knocked out due to the pain. She screams for drugs. It is worth noting that she had no birth plan, or what we'd call one by today's standards. Rebecca and her friend are both in labor in the same room, screaming together, because of a full moon. She uses a 10-count breathing and pushing method for labor.

Social Reactions

Samuel gets pregnancy and labor advice from two friends – one good and one bad. The good advice is from the other dad, the bad advice from his bachelor friend. The female ultrasound doctor tells him to be emotionally supportive and hints that he isn't doing much in that area.

Summary

This movie was made in the mid-1990s which made some of the more obscure pregnancy myths kind of funny. It was weird that the father in the movie was a child psychologist and yet didn't want kids. The only positive for this movie was there was one scene with real dialogue between two men about the actual birth. In this scene, Tom Arnold's character tells Hugh Grant's character that he can watch the videos of his wife's previous births and that they can talk about all the gory stuff. I believe that is more than most men talk about, even if it is only about one small aspect of the birth.

In regards to the fathers' transformation phase in movies, this one did not deviate from the formula. The mother could flip on the parent switch almost instantly, while the dad had to go through a life changing phase from immature bachelor child to kid-ready mature adult. The mother did not have to go through a transformation.

In terms of stereotypes, this movie is full of them. During the birth scene he is panicky, doesn't know what's going on, doesn't keep his wife calm, doesn't offer much support, and gets into a fight with the other father – all in a very short scene. The movie is meant to be funny, which is made apparent in the comedy of errors on the way to the hospital, but the over the top birthing scene just further developed the negative stereotype of the clueless and panicky delivery room father. I believe that this movie does not encourage fathers to want to be assertive at birth.

Juno: Paulie as the biological father, Juno as the biological mother, Mark as the prospective adoptive father, and Vanessa as the adoptive mother. This movie has two fathers in it due to Juno deciding to give her baby up for adoption.

Fathers' Actions

During pregnancy: When Paulie finds out Juno is pregnant, he shows uncertainty as to what to do on all levels. When confronted by Juno as to how he feels about adopting a child, Mark gives an obvious song-and-dance response saying that 'all men want to be a dad'. Mark spends a lot of the movie debating whether or not he does want to be a father. He does read birth books, takes a few classes, and then finally states that he isn't sure if he would even be a good father. Neither Paulie nor Mark go through a transformation. Neither father is present at any prenatal appointments or takes any interest in the stages of the pregnancy.

During labor/birth: Neither Mark nor Paulie are present at the actual birth. Mark has left Vanessa by that time. Juno does not tell Paulie that she has gone into labor, but he figures it out and arrives after it is over.

Mothers' Expectations

During pregnancy: Juno also has the initial denial. There is a lot of talk about abortion, she even visits a clinic. Juno does go through a transformation, but it almost a double one, as she also has to grow up in some of the normal teenage ways. There is brief talk about the physicality of birth, so she knows what to expect when she goes into labor. Vanessa also reads birth books and expects Mark to read them, which he does right away. Vanessa says that, according to the birth books, "Women become mothers when they get

pregnant, and men become fathers when they see the baby."
Vanessa did not go through a transformation, she was ready and
knew what to expect from the start.

During labor/birth: When Juno gives birth, there are no
males there. There are lots of women there, including her best
friend. Juno does want drugs.

Social Reactions

Juno's best friend is supportive of any decision she makes
about the pregnancy and birth. Her parents are also supportive, but
express disappointment about Juno's irresponsibility in getting
pregnant as a young teen.

Summary

Analyzing this movie for its fatherly context proved quite a
challenge since there were two sets of parents. However, both dads
are distant and clueless for almost the entire movie. Mark had to go
through the same transformations as Juno - that of growing up and
accepting future parenthood. Mark stops short and does not even
finish the transformation. Vanessa was the only one who started off
as the same mature and ready woman she ended up as at the end of
the movie.

I won't spend too much time on Paulie's behavior for two
reasons. First, it seemed that Juno kept him at a distance on purpose.
Second, he was in high school. Juno is shown as a young person able
to make very mature decisions on her own, that same character trait
was not shown in Paulie's case. Most of his actions in the movie
were not his fault, or out of his control.

The labor scene was very short. There was no talk about
breastfeeding in this movie, although talks about abortion were
common in the beginning of the movie. There was no dialogue
between any of the three men, Juno's dad, Mark, or Paulie, with
anyone else about the impending birth. The adoptive father Mark's
actions beg to be judged. By the end of the movie he walks away
from fatherhood and marriage so that he can remain a child at heart.
I found it disheartening that neither father was at the birth.

Where the Heart Is: Willy as the biological father, Novalee as the mother, Forney as her boyfriend-to-be and the person who delivers her baby. This movie also has two father figures. There is no separation of the actions during labor and delivery as neither are really shown or dealt with.

Father's Actions

Willy at first refuses to acknowledge the baby's heartbeat, and then abandons his future child and the mother at a random store. Willy shows complete apathy to the pregnancy. This character doesn't have much interaction during the middle of the movie and in relation to the birth. As for Forney, his actions must be examined from just one line in the movie. The nurse who tends to Novalee says that Forney broke through the store window and delivered the baby after she had gone into labor. We can safely assume that he didn't panic and call 911 while standing there like an idiot. I can therefore say that this portrays a positive role model for an assertive male, even if he wasn't the biological father. He also wants to support Novalee and her child in the traditional sense with a stable job. While we do see a transformation of some kind in Willy, we do not see the typical stages of growing up and acceptance of responsibility from Forney. Forney's character is the local librarian, so we can also assume that he was knowledgeable of pregnancy and labor from reading about it, and this was the reason he was able to deliver Novalee's child.

Mother's Expectations

There is not much time spent on the pregnancy in this movie and the delivery scene is not shown. When she wakes up in the hospital after the birth, she is afraid the hospital will take her baby away from her because she can't pay the medical bills.

Social Reactions

One of the characters, Sister Husband, does not treat Novalee like a disabled pregnant woman. She treats Novalee like a normal person. This character also prays for a safe delivery during a lunch with Novalee. Other than that, there are not many reactions to the pregnancy and birth, as they take place early in the movie and mostly off-screen. It is still interesting to note that a male who wasn't the father showed care and stepped into the situation.

Summary

This movie was based on a book written by a woman and directed by a male. There is no real dialogue with any of the parents as to what to expect. The logistics of the pregnancy and birth are dealt with only very briefly, even though where the birth takes place is a major plot point of the movie. I believe this movie is important in the discussion of the role of the father due to the character of Forney. I believe it is impressive for a person to be so assertive in an emergency situation, especially one concerning birth. Forney could have just called 911 and watched, could have just tried to be a labor coach, or just walked away. This is quite a stark contrast to the usual comedy of errors and childish behavior we see from other movie dads. It sets a positive role model for other men, even if the biological father is a deadbeat.

Father of the Bride, Part II: This movie has two fathers and two mothers. George and Nina are the older couple and parents of the other mother Annie. Brian is Annie's husband. The plot centers around a man who initially refuses to accept being a grandfather and also having another child of their own.

Fathers' Actions

<u>During pregnancy</u>: After the initial denial of Nina's pregnancy, George makes it clear that the pregnancy is going to be an interruption of their plans after having all the kids out of the house. He goes through the stereotypical transformation, albeit this time in the grandfather context. He fears the eighteen years after the birth more than the birth itself. George does not offer any dialogue with Brian about what to expect at Annie's birth. Brian is not an

active part of the story, and has minimal parts. George does attend Lamaze classes.

During labor/birth: This is George's third child. He stays calm, comfortable, and organized, even though he does not get much sleep in the days leading up to the labors. Both Nina and Annie go into labor at the same time. He does not panic or act like a buffoon. It is Brian's first child, but Annie's birth takes place off screen, as does Nina's. George is told that Nina must have a C-section, and he still retains his composure, and doesn't really cry either. He apparently did not go to the prenatal appointments. There is also a small comedy of errors in this movie in getting the laboring mothers to the hospital which involves some kind of enema to wake George up.

Mothers' Expectations

During pregnancy: Nina wants George to be happy about the unexpected pregnancy, which in fairness he is after a while. There is no mention of an abortion as an option, and it is apparent she wants to keep it from the start. There is also no talk of breastfeeding between any of the characters. There isn't much talk between George and Nina about expectations, as this seems to be routine by now for them.

During labor/birth: Annie wants her husband there. Nina and Annie are both understanding of the fact that Brian isn't there. George must spend his time between them until Franck, the nursery designer, steps in. As stated earlier, the deliveries happened off-screen without George, so there is not much to comment on.

Social Reactions

There is no real social circle present in this movie, other than the two eccentric wedding planners. They are excited about the pregnancies. One of them, Franck, even goes to the hospital with them (due to the comedy of errors), and overcomes his panic and rises to the occasion to help Annie in the early stages of labor until Brian gets there from work. George and Nina's young son doesn't seem to be too fazed about the new arrival, and their doctor assures them that their age is not too old for new children.

Summary

The birth scenes in this movie are long, but sadly they take place off-screen. George's character is either old-fashioned, or the writers (lots, both men and women), don't want to be controversial. George spends the entire time during both deliveries pacing in the hallway like a father from the 1950s. He also does not show much reaction at the news that his wife has to have a C-section. After the surgery, he calms Nina down with a romantic story about how they met. The gravity of the time right before the active labor is decently portrayed. The doctor in this movie is not demonized like the OB in *Knocked Up*, the Russian OB in *Nine Months*, or the ultrasound tech in *Juno*. I believe this movie is neutral in that neither positive nor negative role models are portrayed. The actions of the father up to the delivery are portrayed well, but there are no delivery room scenes to analyze.

She's Having a Baby: Jake as the father, and Kristy as the mother. Fortunately, this movie only has one set of parents to discuss. Unfortunately, the plot of the movie centers on the transformation that Jake must go through to accept marriage and fatherhood.

Father's Actions

During pregnancy: Jake not only goes through the stereotypical transformation, but it is also set in contrast to his best friend, who refuses to grow up or change. It turns out that Jake had a slight problem with his fertility. He takes offense to this and sets a double standard by not accepting that anything could go wrong with his side of the pregnancy. He then compares himself to a stud horse. He feels that getting her pregnant and becoming a father is an obligation. Even though the pregnancy was planned, he is still not happy with the news. He fights depression as the pregnancy progresses. He does take a birth class with Kristy. He is still going through his transformation up until Kristy goes into labor.

During labor/birth: There isn't a comedy of errors in the strict sense in this movie. However, when she says it is time to go to the hospital, he panics. He actually forgets and leaves her at the front door while he leaves in the car. Jake does try to keep her calm on the way to the hospital. He bumbles a bit at first in the hospital, but does finally come to terms with the situation and does his best to be mature and help Kristy. He times her contractions during what appears to be pre-labor. Something goes wrong during the labor and he is forced outside the delivery room. The final stage of his transformation is when he is given bad news that his wife and child are in danger. He breaks down and cries after given the news and when Kristy goes into surgery. At the end of the movie, Jake tells Kristy that he is done writing his book about the transformation that the main character went through when his wife had a child.

Mother's Expectations

During pregnancy: At times this movie portrays Kristy as a negative stereotype. Many of Jake and Kristy's scenes together are during fights and arguments. She is very emotional in many scenes. She wants Jake to be as happy as her about the prospect of having a child. Kristy comes off at times as being manipulative by not telling him that she went off the pill. She tells Jake that she wants him to be more mature about things in their life.

During labor/birth: Kristy gives birth on her back with her feet in stirrups. A male OB does her counting for her. Her breathing almost makes her hyperventilate, so it might have been old-school (1970s) Lamaze. She seems to be unable to cope with the pain, and screams that she can't stop pushing even when the OB tells her to stop. The medical staff then proceeds to knock her out with gas. She then obviously has a C-section; no consent is shown to have been given.

Social Reactions

There is a scene where both Jake's and Kristy's parents are sitting around a table discussing having a child. There is some talk among the parents about the logistics of birth. We actually see

Kristy's mom using a scare tactic by talking about all the problems she had at birth, and how that it wasn't a very good experience. Her mother talks about her hips being too small, the pain being horrible, that the baby was breech, and how she almost lost the baby. Kristy's dad casually mentions that he was out playing golf during labor. Her dad also talks about the financial responsibility of an infant. Even though this technically counts as dialogue about the impending birth, the advice is very poor.

Summary

Of all the movies reviewed, I believe this one sets the worst standard as to what a father should expect, and what he should do during the labor. Fear is a small factor during the pregnancy and a major factor during the birth. The OB in the delivery room did not come off as empathetic. No consent was shown as being given in the movie. Breech birth was presented as an emergency situation, even though that is now known to be a normal birth position by almost all midwives. I believe this movie sets parents up to be passive and submissive in whatever the medical staff tells them to do. The father is a bad role model for those who wish to be more assertive. Jake's intentions after the transformation were good. However, the hospital's actions being presented as acceptable or routine is very disheartening.

Thumbs up or down?

The authors of these movies were both men and women, collectively. It is interesting to note that *Nine Months*, *She's Having a Baby*, and *Knocked Up* were written and directed by men. *Juno* was written by a woman. *Father of the Bride, Part II* was written by many writers, both men and women. *Where the Heart Is* was written by a woman. The comedy of errors seems to be a formula for the movies written by the men. It is odd how abortion is more acceptable to talk about than breastfeeding, as some of the movies have the parents discuss it openly.

All the movie fathers, with the exception of Forney in *Where the Heart Is*, go through a transformation. They always start out as men with traits such as immaturity, fear, lack of knowledge, desire, or simply just not father material – and then undergo a personal transformation into mature men who are ready and willing, even desiring to be a parent. The exception here is Mark from *Juno* who doesn't even complete that transformation formula. To put men in this light is very dangerous. As I stated in the beginning – either men act this way, or a few are influenced by what they see. Neither observation is acceptable.

The stereotypes portrayed in some of these movies hinder fathers in a number of ways. Some will not want to be a bumbling idiot. Others will not want to be perceived as an idiot even if they know what they are doing and what is going on. This will turn off fathers before they even start. Some fathers-to-be out there will not want to deal with the way some of the women are portrayed either. To imply that a father is inadequate on the whole and must have a life-altering identity change to be a good father is extremely unfair.

On the flip side, the positive role models may help to dispel the negative stereotypes in the other movies. Ben from *Knocked Up* is a good example. That character is more likely to inspire a man to be a very involved father or to show that fathers like them can exist. These movies shed some light on what is expected of men during childbirth. Let us hope that those portrayals continue to evolve and show fathers as more knowledgeable and assertive.

Yes, most first time fathers most likely will go through a transformation, but not all of those first time fathers start out as fifteen year old idiots. For many fathers, this transformation is a healthy and functional process. As for second time fathers and so on, these transformations have most likely already taken place, and there is even more time now for the adaptation and perfection of their functions during birth.

Chapter Seven
Fathers and Birth in Print,
Part 1: Roles in magazines,
newspapers, and the Internet

Are newspapers still fifty cents?

Since this chapter is about magazine and newspaper articles, and internet sources that were directed at dads about birth – I do not feel that it is important who wrote the articles or books. They only needed to include a significant amount of information aimed at the father during childbirth. That means I did not review sources that were written for women only, as that would make this chapter impossibly long. Medical books were also not considered.

My purpose is not to show the chaos or overwhelming amount of material that needs to be read, but to show fathers that they have the resources to examine or create their desired roles. I also wanted to offer some examples which best represented the spectrum of all the types of printed sources out there. In essence, fathers at birth may not know about the journalistic microscope they are under, let alone where to look for these types of solutions to their dilemmas during the birthing hour.

The focus of this chapter is a bit old-fashioned, but I feel that it must be covered regardless. I also must make the disclaimer that some of my summaries of articles may be very opinionated. Keep in mind that these sources are being analyzed in a very specific scope, that of their usefulness for fathers to strengthen their presence in the delivery room, and that my summaries may not always reflect the quality of the source as a whole.

In the previous chapter, we asked a certain set of questions when watching the fathers in birth scenes at movies. For this chapter, we can also keep a certain set of questions in mind when reading written sources:

- What is the message or point that the author is trying to convey?
- Does the author succeed in conveying that message?
- Does this article present any new insights or information for fathers developing roles?
- What are the important points of the article?
- Does the article help or hinder both positive and negative role models, as well as the redefining of the roles of the father at birth?

We have a paperboy?

Our first article comes from the *Washington Post*. It was written by Ranit Mishori, and was in the July 4, 2006 edition. The title is "Feeling Her Pain: Intensity of Childbirth Experience Leaves Some Men Feeling Ill-prepared."[43]

The article starts out describing how most fathers are expected to be at their child's birth in today's society. The article brings up the question - what about fathers who can't handle the situation? Now that fathers are obligated to be at the birth of their child regardless of their desires, knowledge, and opinions concerning childbirth – there are starting to be negative side effects. The stress on the father seems to have increased, and sometimes this affects the laboring woman.

The article draws many of its conclusions from an academic study done by Judith Leavitt, titled "What Do Men Have to Do with It?" According to that study, over the past few decades, fathers at birth have been forced into a new high-pressure situation without any real preparation or training. Furthermore, there is almost no research on the expectations, opinions, and reactions of fathers being at a birth to draw upon. Two other different studies by different medical journals showed reactions in which men expressed helplessness, acute fear, anxiety, frustration, difficulty, and uncertainty attending labor.

---

[43] "Feeling Her Pain," The Washington Post, last modified July 4, 2006 , http://www.washingtonpost.com/wp-dyn/content/article/2006/07/03/AR2006070300790.html

According to Leavitt, by the mid-1980s, it was the social norm for fathers to be in attendance during labor in hospitals. There is no mention of out of hospital births in this article. Yet twenty-five years later, there are still only a few prenatal classes geared towards men attending a vaginal birth. The classes on attending a C-section are almost non-existent. In this article, the stage is very clearly set for the average father being ill-prepared for almost all of the non-traditional, and even sometimes the traditional, birth.

What follows is the discussion of the obvious split in opinion now concerning this awkward situation. Some experts say that men should go back to the waiting room or hallway. Others want more classes for men. Quotes are shown by various experts on how specialized classes geared towards the father and not the mother, tend to lower the overall negative reactions from men who attend birth. Another chief concern from many fathers is seeing their wife differently after witnessing the physical birth. It takes time for some men to want to return to the sex life they had previous to the birth.

The article concludes with a quote by David Downing, an obstetrician at Washington Hospital Center. Downing says that even the best preparation only goes so far. He then says, "First time dads really have no clue." For readers of this book, however, this is not a new conclusion. It is refreshing to find more sources that are attempting to bring this unfortunate situation to the forefront of our societies' attention.

Some useful, perhaps new, information gleaned from the article for fathers wishing to assert themselves and define their roles at birth is that more and more hospitals are offering prenatal classes for men. Even if the content of those classes may be off base, for example, by focusing too much on the emotional aspect – at least the effort is being made. Changes to the class format can always be altered after the fact.

The most important focus of this article is the discussion of the social obligation of dad's being in the delivery room. Basically, this means that some fathers are still not comfortable being at the birth. The preparation part of the fathers at birth movement has not caught up with the social demands of how they attend births.

I do not think that this article either helps or hinders those men out there who want to re-establish their roles during labor. This author describes the water the father is drowning in, but does not throw a rope by offering any solutions. I hope that I can successfully remedy this pattern by the end of this book.

Our second article comes from *Time Magazine*. The title is "Daddy Boot Camp" by Jeninne Lee-St. John and was printed in the June 5, 2008 edition.[44]

The article starts off very bluntly with a quote from Steve Dubin stating that the social view of dads is that of a bumbling fool. He and another person, Darryl Wooten, teach a class directed at men who will soon become fathers. Tips for childbirth are only one of the many focuses of this course; others being stress management, diaper tips, and basic infant care. The class was created by a man named Greg Bishop in 1990 after people kept asking him for tips concerning birth and early parenting.

When it comes to the actual philosophies of this class, it claims to challenge old stereotypes where the father was gladly removed from the birth and infant rearing duties. The notion that fathers can't be useful for births and infant care is also confronted. New students who attend the class are actually given real infants to get comfortable with, from other dad volunteers. The focus is not only on what is expected of men, but what men want as well. A platform is presented where men can give feedback during class discussions.

Other factors that are stressed are the importance of communication with the mother, dealing with feelings of helplessness, and when the mother's sex life can return to normal (not that the men were trying to rush it, but as a matter of safety). The article ends on the disappointing note that even in this class, attendance is not always the man's idea. Roughly half of the participants claim that they were asked by the soon-to-be mother to attend the class.

---

[44] "Daddy Boot Camp," Time Magazine, last modified June 5, 2008,
    http://www.time.com/time/magazine/article/0,9171,1812052,00.html

I found a few new insights in this piece that were very interesting. I found it unusual, but still useful, that Spike TV did a survey of 1,000 dads and that 71% felt they had to start from scratch about how they were going to handle the birth. I also did not know that the creator of this class wrote a book called *A Crash Course for New Dads*. I was not encouraged by the fact that this class has been around since 1990, yet I had not heard of it nor the creator's book until this article came up in my Internet search.

I feel that there were many important points stressed in the article. It's a great idea that volunteers bring in their infants, stunt babies, for prospective dads to get used to handling. The notion that it is not a one-way lecture class and fosters dialogue between men about the actual birth is very encouraging. Dialogue is the name of the game in the strategy of keeping men involved in the long run. Stereotypes are addressed, and new role models are discussed. I believe this class greatly helps the efforts of fathers wishing to re-establish their roles during childbirth.

Our third article comes from the Jan-Feb, 2007 issue of *Mothering* magazine, titled "You Want to Give Birth Where?" by Michael Robertson.[45]

This article starts like a birth story. However, it differs from many of the usual birth stories in that it talks about a transformation, and luckily enough, the father/author does not begin that transformation as a blundering teenage-minded idiot. He writes about the journey where he originally views homebirth as a radical and fringe movement and then changes his mind gradually to view it as something that everyone, who is low risk anyway, should be doing.

I found the article enlightening in that the transformation that the author went through was gradual, over a four year time period, and not rushed at the last minute like so many media and Hollywood representations. He spent many years constructively communicating and talking with his wife about her desires, fears, and what kind birth she wanted. Once she convinced him that she

---

[45] Michael Robertson, "You Want to Give Birth Where?" *Mothering*, Issue 140, January/February, 2007

wanted a home birth, he adjusted his attitude maturely and appropriately and found very useful ways to help with the labor.

This is a very useful article for those who wish to develop their own roles for pregnancy and especially birth by not only showing someone else actually doing it, but the author takes time to explain how things happened. This article is a great example of how to turn a birth story into a useful dialogue for other would-be fathers to learn from.

Our fourth article comes from the magazine *Midwifery Today*. It is titled "Papatoto: Homebirth from a Father's Perspective", by Michael Welch. [46]

This is a relatively short article in which the author uses very descriptive language to talk about his fears during the birth and pregnancy. He talks about how hard it is to emotionally relate to a woman when one is not a woman, and how fears and uncertainty can sometime be overwhelming during birth. However, the author rises to the occasion and helps his wife emotionally through the dark parts of labor and also connects with the baby.

The thing that jumped out right away was that this father had his best friend help him with the home birth. Even though the article itself glossed over that seemingly unimportant note, it was hugely significant to me. His friend Jim was helping by making food and drinks that the wife wanted during labor, and it is safe to assume he was helping with other small tasks around the house. Not only was the father there to assist his wife, there was another male there to assist the father!

This article, even though it may be yet another birth story, can have a huge impact on the development of roles for fathers at birth. In essence, there are many women out there who get to attend a birth before they have their first child, and therefore get an idea of what may happen at theirs. I don't know if the father's friend in this story had children of his own yet, but I like the idea of fathers having the occasional chance to attend a birth that is not their own, so that they too can get a sense of the atmosphere and energy surrounding a

---

[46] Michael Welch, "Papatoto: Homebirth from a Father's Perspective," *Midwifery Today*, Issue 58, Summer, 2001, http://www.midwiferytoday.com/articles/papatoto.asp

birth. This article is a very useful in that it shows that a situation like that is not abnormal, and can even have possible benefits.

Our fifth article is from a Canadian newspaper, the *Vancouver Sun*, and is titled "Fathers-To-Be Asked to Wait Outside: Study Looks at Trends in Labour and Delivery, How They Affect Rate of C-Sections," by Sharon Kirky.[47]

This article is a bit hard to follow, as it jumps back and forth between statistics, quotes, and possible trends in reaction to those same statistics and quotes. The bulk of the writing is about examining all of the usual birth intervention methods and whether or not they have decreased or increased in certain Canadian hospitals. Somewhere in that mix is that the percentage of fathers in the delivery room, in certain Canadian hospitals, has gone down 7 percent or so in recent years.

Even though the article may get confusing at times, it does make one observation clear. Hospitals are starting to discourage fathers from being present during labor, even though there are multiple studies that show they are beneficial to the mother and birth. It does not venture a guess as to why Canadian hospitals may be doing this, except for one brief reference to a SARS outbreak in 2004 keeping many people out of labor rooms.

Our sixth article is from a United Kingdom newspaper called *The Guardian* entitled "When It Comes to Childbirth, Some Fathers Are Having Kittens," by Lucy Atkins.[48]

This is an excellent article that delves into what happens when it is mandatory or obligatory for all fathers to attend their wife's birth. It successfully makes the case that there are fathers out there who are simply not meant to be at birth. Either the father may not want to be there, or the mother may not want the father there. Luckily, the article does not go into why these types of choices may

---

[47] Sharon Kirkey, "Fathers-to-be asked to wait outside: Study looks at trends in labour and delivery, how they affect rate of C-Sections," *The Vancouver Sun*, last modified December 15, 2011, http://www2.canada.com/vancouversun/news/archives/story.html?id=c09dd9dd-6bf5-4c48-a441-96909c18a06a

[48] Lucy Atkins, "When it comes to childbirth, some fathers are having kittens," *The Guardian*, last modified June 21, 2006, http://www.guardian.co.uk/lifeandstyle/2006/jun/22/familyandrelationships.health

be made. The article goes on to list many of the ways that certain fathers can be a hindrance to the laboring mother.

More importantly, the author makes the reasonable assertion that one of the main reasons that fathers aren't of much help during labor is that they aren't sure what they should do. The basic coaching methods can get tiring and annoying after a while. It concludes that mothers should be the first to decide if they want their husbands present during birth, and then that the dad must find ways to be active and supportive.

I could not agree more with almost all that the article discusses. It starts to lay out the first steps for fathers to develop roles. The article recognized a problem, discussed some of the reasons, and then even offered solutions. Reading this is very beneficial for fathers who wish to adapt or develop roles in that it offers one of the first steps in that direction. It brings attention to the purpose of this book, and helps develop answers.

Our last article is from another UK newspaper, *The Independent*, with an article titled "Fathers In Hard Labour: 'Being There' During Childbirth Is Not Automatically A Good Thing," by David Shannon.[49]

This article differs from the prior two by delving right into research done with the fathers themselves to see how they felt, whereas the article by Lucy Atkins deals with men at birth from more of a woman's point of view. In this piece by David Shannon, much of it is spent talking to fathers who did not have the picture perfect reaction to the birth of their child. Some men felt useless, some men felt guilty of the social obligation to be there, and some men felt they were holding their wives back.

The author then goes on to discuss some brief history of the introduction of men into the delivery room, and also the very real dangers of socially obligating a father to attend birth. Basically, forcing a father to attend a birth can have very real negative effects

---

[49] David Shannon, "Fathers in hard labour: 'Being there' during childbirth is not automatically a good thing," *The Independent*, last modified October 24, 1993, http://www.independent.co.uk/life-style/fathers-in-hard-labour-being-there-during-childbirth-is-not-automatically-a-good-thing-david-shannon-reports-1512817.html

on both the mother and father. However, it stops short of a one way discussion by stating that for the large majority of couples, the father being present at labor is beneficial to the mother. The article concludes with the assertion that true consent by both parents for the father's inclusion in the birth should not be assumed, but carefully discussed by both mother and father long before the actual birth.

This article is also very useful in that it considered attitudes from men about birth, and not solely in the form of birth stories. Birth stories can offer glimpses of how the father felt during birth. However, this article goes far beyond that and looks for patterns. The article finds them in examples such as uncertainty, anxiety, and guilt.

These last three articles are useful for guarding against complacency. They are not the first, nor will they be the last articles that discuss the extremely new trend of removing the father from the delivery room once again, after many battles to get them in over the last 30 or 40 years. I like to think of it as a reminder that even if one has chosen to adapt or develop a role for labor, there may still be resistance from society.

If anything, these last three articles bring to attention the very urgent need to further develop and establish fathers' roles during birth. It is no longer acceptable to be at your wife's side simply being emotionally supportive. Fathers can do that and much more.

I believe that all of these newspaper and magazine articles are sufficient cross-samples to bring to light one very important topic. All seven articles have one thing in common: dissatisfaction with the current situation, the status quo, of fathers and their actions and expectations during birth. There are people who wish to change that and there are others who seek to study why this is the case. I want to offer tools to remedy the entire enigma.

Gutenberg had a computer?

In the last section, we analyzed newspaper and magazine articles that related to dads and childbirth. It is important to ask what the difference is between what is found in online articles and what is found on websites. The main difference is that content written in articles is static and unchanging. Ideas, information, and preconceived notions are put down in a very permanent format. The only way to change what is presented is to release a new edition with corrections or additions.

Websites are dynamic and interactive. Information is constantly updated. Ideas are continually developed. Preconceived notions are constructively challenged so that they can adapt, change, or be reinforced. Unfortunately, this is happening at a crawl, if at all, for the content relating to birthing roles for fathers.

Where we have already discussed the views of large scale organizations – this chapter focuses on more grassroots oriented websites, and their goals and methods. I didn't discuss the organizations' goals and methods in the other chapter, I just presented their official stances to show how chaotic the field is. On the other hand, internet resources show us what is out there in regards to what is more proactive and what can change day to day.

In order to best understand the power and effects of the Internet, we can look at the history of the printing press. Johann Gutenberg perfected the printing press around 1440, and its applications and use forever changed Europe and the rest of the world. Books that were not readily available or common flooded the population. Compared to the speed of delivery and information corrections of the printing press, it is no stretch of the imagination to say that the effects of the Information Age will be much more remarkable.

Many people have noticed the similarities between the effects of the printing press and the effects of the Internet on the spreading of information and ideas. In 1998, James A. Dewar had the foresight to analyze these two similar technological advances in a Rand publication titled *The Information Age and the Printing Press: Looking Backward to See Ahead.*[50] He summarizes this view: "There

---

[50] "The Information Age and the Printing Press: Looking Backward to See Ahead," Rand Corporation. Last modified September 15, 2010.
http://www.rand.org/pubs/papers/P8014/index2.html

are some provocative parallels between the communications changes enabled by networked computers and those enabled by the printing press in its early days. Each defining technology represents an important breakthrough in the ability of humans to communicate with each other; each enables important changes in how we preserve, update and disseminate knowledge; how we retrieve knowledge; the ownership of knowledge; and how we acquire knowledge."

Just like the printing press, the Internet will have the same repercussions, but only exponentially more powerful. Dewar states earlier in his essay that "changes in the Information Age will be as dramatic as those in the Middle Ages in Europe. The printing press has been implicated in the Reformation, the Renaissance and the Scientific Revolution, all of which had profound effects on their eras; similarly profound changes may already be underway in the information age."

To put it more bluntly - printed materials are snapshots, online materials are living documents. Therefore, one must ask a very different set of questions when reviewing a website for useful or relevant information that can be used for role development and perhaps for childbirth in general. Here are some examples:

- Are they really just shorter examples of what is usually found in the basic books or magazines?
- Does the site offer a place for exchanges and dialogue, like a message board or a forum?
- Do they just offer different summaries of pregnancy related information?
- Is it a website only for dads and pregnancy/birth?
- Is it a website that advertises a book or video, related to birth, with or without dads?
- Is it a website that is related to birth topics in general, and has articles for dads?
- Is it a random website, with a dad-related birth article?
- Is it a collection of birth stories, with some written by dads?
- Does the site even consider new or better roles, or just offer places to rehash general pregnancy information?

- Is the site for an organization, a movement, a collection of birth stories, or an educational source?
- Does the site combine resources for the comparison and contrasting of different roles for the goal of better developing them?

I am not judging the website as a whole, just in the search for very specific information. Once these questions are answered, we can then evaluate the content on its value for dads. The printing press was an explosion of information, and yet we only got Reynalde and Soranus from that movement for our purposes. I am hopeful that the Internet explosion will yield more than that. I believe that there should be more.

I rated the websites on three points. The first was for general pregnancy information. The second point was for presentation of new or useful information on the birth stage only. Finally, it was judged as interactive or not. Not being interactive is not necessarily a negative observation, as some websites are simply for advertising a book or DVD. It is only a negative judgment if the website claims to be interactive or a source of references and resources – and it isn't.

I decided to leave out basic social networking sites. These websites are too interactive. They change too fast, and sometimes include more opinion than honest inquiry. Parenting.com, Parentlink.com, and Mothering.com had very little content for expecting dads, so they do not need a review here. Unlike the three just listed, there are some websites I consider shorts, in that they had some basic introductory information for fathers on pregnancy in general. Here are some examples of links that had little to no information:

- **Greatdad.com/forum** - basic pregnancy information.
- **www.dadmag.com** - nothing about birth, or even general pregnancy information, using the internal search.
- **Edads.com** - also nothing about birth, using the internal search.
- **www.homebirthdads.com** - this is only very brief advertisement for a video of the same name.

- www.newdadssurvivalguide.comindex.html - also a book.
- www.imgoingtobeadad.com.au - weekly email updates on what happens during the pregnancy.
- www.babycenter.com - nothing real for dads, pregnancy, birth, or otherwise.

I decided to review five websites that had developed content that fathers could use for consideration of their function during labor. This list is not all inconclusive of everything on the web, but I feel it is a sufficient representation.

www.fathersonline.com: This site basically seemed destined only for very specific questions and answers. It is very much a chaotic free for all. To be honest, I had no desire to read through the endless stream of random information requests. This place represents the pendulum swinging too far in the other direction for our direct purposes. This link will have no rating, as the website doesn't stand up to searching very well. It is a good place to go if you want an immediate online answer about something that someone else might know specifically. It is very interactive, but perhaps too much so.

www.mrdad.com: This is Armin Brott's website, and after reading his book I was eager to look through it. However, the site's main concern is to promote his books. It has a FAQ for expectant fathers, with some decent but general answers. There is no real pregnancy or birth information, as this is obviously presented in his books. There are no articles. There is a very good links and resources section. This website is also relatively small. This isn't necessarily bad, since his books are really good. This website is mediocre when it came to general pregnancy information. There was no real acknowledgment about the importance of the birth stage itself. This website is not interactive, unless you count the link to his radio show where you can ask him questions.

fatherstobe.org: This website is mainly a large review for the author's book on general pregnancy information. It is more of a proactive website by having webinars. There are links to other DVDs, a few related internet videos, and some magazine article links. There is a newsletter, information on conferences, but no articles.

There are not even snippets from any books, just reviews and introductions. There are no real references to fathers at the actual birth. The whole website is a very complex online advertisement. It is not very interactive.

www.fathers.com: This is a very user friendly pregnancy and beyond site. There are some good research based articles and they offer online communities and events. This site does have the unique attitude of trying to develop fathers in other just as important aspects, such as raising kids in different types of settings. Even if there are not developments focused on functions during birth, the first baby steps are there. I did find one article that had a very good quote which strikes to the heart of the matter that this book is addressing: "The quality of the birth experience influences the quality of your relationship with your family." I could not put this better myself. This was a very good website for trying to add new pregnancy information, not just rehash it. There are lots of recognitions of the father's usefulness during the birthing stage.

birthnavigators.wordpress.com: This site is directed at birthing couples, and seems more cutting edge than most. It is actually a blog, even though it doesn't look like one at first. It does not have a links or resources section per se, but there are some included throughout the site. This is the first website where I saw a 'feature films to watch' section, which suggested two birth related movies that can be watched on the Internet. It also has a News section where current events related to childbirth are updated. It also has an email subscription option that was encouraging to see.

On its About page is this quote: "The posts are written to stir thought about how to improve the American health care system and to educate men as to their role and participation in this most exciting event in life." This quote implies that there is a standard, it just simply must be taught. While I disagree with the implication of a current standard, at least it is open minded about it by trying to promote thoughts and opinions.

There are also articles, at least two that discuss men and pregnancy and birth, which was a refreshing sight. Its main function doesn't seem to be rehashing pregnancy information that is already out there; it seems like it is attempting to add to it. I also get the sense that the website is seeking to add to current ideas; the gap of solid roles for expecting fathers is directly addressed. It is as interactive as a blog can be.

www.fathersforum.com: This website features a book, a DVD, articles, and classes (although only in the Berkeley, CA area). There is an online group that anyone can join. The links and resources section is very good. There is a very strong focus on support groups and dialogue. There are no efforts for the development of standards or guidelines concerning what men should do during labor.

In the articles section, there is one about pregnancy and birth, written by the author of the website. In it, I found some excellent quotes:

"Helping choose the birth attendants, midwife or doctor, and being involved in the choice of where the baby will be born is another way men begin becoming involved."

"Fathers who are able to participate in the birth of their child often report that the sharing of this experience with their partner/wife remains one of the most important moments in their relationship and in their lives. Even if the birth is difficult or a cesarean delivery, men still feel strongly about being together at this special time. Fathers' importance in participating at the birth is finally getting the acknowledgment it deserves."

"Expectant fathers also need to explore what they need at the birth. What kind of support does the expectant dad need to ask for? Many of the new fathers I have worked with talked about how important having a male friend available for them was."

This is very useful, as before then it didn't occur to me to think about what men wanted during labor. I can now say that it is probably to be useful, important, and involved. Information, knowledge, and the power of choice are also most likely desired. It is nice to see another very involved father calling out for the need for further exploration, even if it's about their own needs. Even though the large majority of the article is about the pregnancy and post-birth periods, he does pose good questions at the end of his article, and acknowledges the need for more involvement during labor by fathers. This website was both interactive and not. It supported local in-person meetings, but nothing online.

I don't want this chapter to be a useless and glorified Internet review. There are other places that can do that. This chapter serves the function of displaying just enough sources to show how there is no consensus of the roles, or the need for their development, on the Internet. I found some websites that were really good, in-depth, and interactive. They had some very good pregnancy information. However, some only acknowledged that something is lacking. I took these notes so that later people may set the stage for a more ideal website.

It is very easy for some people to criticize something without offering some constructive feedback. What I was hoping to find is a website with these criteria:

- One or two links with basic, yet thorough, pregnancy information.
- A section each for the obvious: links, books, articles.
- A forum where fathers can seek out others privately, for one on one answers.
- A mailing list for new articles/books/info.
- And most importantly, a forum where newly proposed roles could have a section of their own for comment, feedback, and constructive criticisms.

By now, most are thinking: OK, we get it; there is nothing out there, *in any medium* that deals with the gap and tries to fill it. While that might at times seem like an obsession, I also want to point out that these books, websites, and other resources are the materials that I had to use when designing my proposed roles. I want to show others what I drew from so that they may also do the same as I did and use what is out there to come up with their own roles.

Dewar states that the effects of the Internet on information will be tremendous. I think we can use some of that momentum to focus new energy into role development for fathers during labor. We know that it can happen, as Tosh stated earlier that changes of how science viewed the biological processes of birth helped to challenge previous patriarchal and Christian based ideas about women and birth. Changes like that will happen today, and we must act on it now to mold them better.

Chapter Eight
Fathers and Birth in Print,
Part 2: Roles in books

How did we read before the Internet?

At this point, we have evaluated brief references to the evolution of the stances of fathers and physicians on birth. The Greek father viewed childbirth a mystical event, involving the same fluids as death. With the inclusion of anatomy, Roman physicians and fathers viewed their part in the birth as the biological fulfillment of their patriarchal place in the universe. By the time of Reynalde, birth was changing into a biological event for the mother as well, with fathers now unsure of their part to play. When we arrive at the present, birth was stripped of all other aspects, including the biological. It was distilled down to a strictly medical event, to take place in a hospital, with the father as a mere attendant in varying capacities.

Richard K. Reed makes this clear on page 134 of his book *Birthing Fathers: The Transformation of Men in American Rites of Birth*: "The alternative birthing movement sought to reintegrate social relations, psychological experiences, and spiritual awareness back into birth. However when push came to shove, hospitals and physicians opted for biological birth over holistic birthing, and chose Lamaze over Dick-Read and Bradley. This maintains hospital standards of efficiency and effectiveness, without disrupting the practice of birth or the power structure of hospital birthing. Fathers are admitted, but only to facilitate the biological process of birth and empower the existing institution in relations to the patient."

The above quote makes us ask many questions, and most of these questions can be answered by the books that deal with childbirth. What is the biological model, and how did it come to be the rule administered by hospitals? Who are Lamaze, Bradley, and Dick-Read? What was the alternative birthing movement? Are there authors that challenge or agree with these and others authors like them?

When we ask these questions, we also arrive at the discussion of fathers in print, especially books. Asking these questions throws the door wide open for the review of almost all the books printed in the last 100 years, and more specifically, those books that had any focus on the father's function during birth.

When starting this project, I had to start from scratch, which also happens to be the issue facing all other first time fathers out there. My goal was to read as many books for fathers as I could so that others didn't have to. This way, I could present the best and worst, and finally, use what was missing for the development of my new roles.

As a side note, I'm sure I've read the majority of dads' birthing books; it is a small niche. I am also sure some were missed. No one wants to read a bunch of mini-book reports. I will talk about a few books that stood out, for better or worse, and of the many things I learned while diving into this topic.

How old is the oldest birth book?

When discussing any type of role, for both the mother and father, I started with the obvious route, the various birthing methods out there. Some of them did not discuss fathers at all, others were directed at couples, and some were directed at fathers in particular. Let me say now that I am not putting forth any birthing method as better than another. I am also not judging the author or the method as a whole, but only for the strict context of content that hinders or helps fathers who want to further develop roles. Let's start with the five most popular, in order of publication and research.

Grantly Dick-Read, *Childbirth Without Fear* (1944). In Dick-Read's original book, there is a short chapter on fathers, but only for them to understand the biological process so as to not get confused and in the way. The passage that I found most interesting was in the chapter 'A Philosophy of Childbirth': "The philosophy of childbirth is in the reality of its spiritual manifestations and the incomprehensible miracle of its mechanism - familiarity with its natural performance directs our minds to a closer understanding of human nature and conduct."[51]

If I had to point to a paragraph that started it all, that would be it. The spirituality of childbirth is a result of its biological function. We may also make further observations about human nature by the understanding of the mechanism of birth. It is remarkable to witness how a few sentences can have huge ramifications decades later.

The "Bradley Birth Method", by Robert A. Bradley, published in *Husband Coached Childbirth* (1965).

The book borders on being an infomercial, offering little substance to fathers of what to actually do at the birth, instead just telling people to take his class to find out more. He does talk about his epiphanies and philosophies a good deal in between telling prospective parents to take his birth classes.

Here is the opening paragraph from Chapter Two, "The Theory of Childbirth":

"To anyone like myself who grew up in God's great outdoors and witnesses the birth process in domesticated and non-domesticated animals, other than human, the inevitable question is bound to arise: Why do all other animals peacefully and joyfully give birth unassisted? Why can't the human animal do this? What makes the difference?

"Throughout my childhood I was fortunate enough to live on the outskirts of a small town in what amounted to a farming environment. We had a large barn that in the course of years was occupied by many domestic animals. We averaged from eight to ten cats, had horses, cows, goats, and a succession of dogs. In addition to these domestic animals, the open countryside adjacent to our place afforded the opportunity to observe many animals in the wild. The birth processes I witnessed in these many creatures showed no objective evidence of pain or suffering. The opposite was true: The animal mother's eyes were radiant with joy and happiness."[52]

---

[51] Dick-Read, Grantly, *Childbirth Without Fear*, 2nd rev. ed., (New York: Harper Brothers, 1944), 25.

At first glance, this seems like a reasonable and well thought out philosophy. I even tend to agree with it, mostly. However, after giving it a little more thought, there is a glaring flaw in Bradley's logic. It is most likely true that animals everywhere can have unassisted and pain-free birth.

Bradley does not take his logical train of thought to its next extremely obvious step. If he claims that his method teaches humans to birth like mammals out in nature, which it could very well do, then there would be no need for hospitals. Following his logic, all animals should give birth in hospitals, assisted by an OB or physician; or all humans who learn his method should give birth unassisted and outside of hospitals. It has to be one or the other according to his philosophy. How this logical conclusion has been overlooked is interesting in and of itself, but I will not go into it any further here.

On a side note, both Bradley and Dick-Read were proponents against twilight birth, in which the laboring mother was knocked out, and the baby was delivered by the physician. This was done so that the mother may not know of the agony of delivering a baby. The alternative birthing revolution was in started in contrast to this type of birth that was common in hospitals during the early 20th century.

Dr. Fernand Lamaze, *The Lamaze Birth Method*. It is difficult to discuss this birth method, as Fernand Lamaze did not actually write any books himself, and has no true publication date. He observed a new and unique birthing method in Russia, and then started practicing it himself in France. A mother he attended to wrote a book called *Thank you, Dr. Lamaze*, which then spawned a movement and an organization dedicated to teaching his method. The particulars of his method can best be summarized from their website:

"In 1951, Dr. Fernand Lamaze introduced a method of childbirth in France by incorporating techniques he observed in Russia. This method, consisting of childbirth education classes, relaxation, breathing techniques and continuous emotional

---

[52] Bradley, Robert A., *Husband Coached Childbirth*, rev. ed., (New York: Harper and Row, Publisher, 1974), 8.

support from the father and a specially trained nurse, became known as 'the Lamaze method.'"[53]

Based on the comparisons made by many other authors, there were only minor differences between this method and the Bradley and Dick-Read methods. Granted, there are subtle differences in the types of emotional support and variances in the breathing techniques used by all of the other birth methods out there, but to go into Lamaze any further would be splitting hairs. Since he did not write a sourcebook himself, we cannot discuss his philosophical views the same way we can with Bradley and later, Odent.

Frederick LeBoyer, *Birth Without Violence* (1975). This book is in an unusual prose format, almost like a poem. It is relatively short, and at times it is hard to follow. In Section Three of LeBoyer's book, he talks about the wholeness of nature, while at the same time talking about the hospital attendants at the birth. He makes little to no reference to the fathers and their functions. His main philosophy centers more on the child being born than the laboring mother. He feels that infants should be born into warmth and darkness, not a cold room and glaring lights. His birth method attempts to deviate from the sterile hospital settings into more ambient delivery rooms.

Michel Odent, *Birth Reborn* (1984). This doctor focuses on opposing unnecessary medical intervention. In this book, he intricately describes the cozy atmosphere that he has created in his clinic. He has created a room that looks exactly like a person's home bedroom, and then adopts a midwife model to use in that setting.

He does compare and contrast the finer points of his methods to Dick-Read and LeBoyer in his book. Odent also disagrees with Bradley in that women did not forget their instincts on normal birthing. That brings up another huge philosophical flaw. If the medical staff is for necessary interventions only and a maternity ward should be created to look like someone's home, then why continue to advocate hospital births over home births? That seems extremely counterintuitive to me. Odent attempts to put the power

---

[53] "History," Lamaze International, accessed December 7, 2013, http://www.lamaze.org/WhoWeAre/History/tabid/104/Default.aspx

of birth back into women's hands, but not in their homes, only his clinic. I still like the book for its attitude and many of its conclusions, but that philosophical flaw is almost too much to bear.

I only go into their philosophies briefly, as the rest of their books either further delve into philosophical musing, or it swings the pendulum full scale and goes into the strictly biological. My short summaries are not meant to be damning, it is just that Richard Reed summarizes the authors much better than me. Also, this book is reflected off of Reed's research as well.

I believe Reed's summary of the alternative birthing revolution that resulted from these five practitioners is the best. "The birthing revolution taught American men that they could protect their women from fear and pain of birth. Many fathers tried to defend birthing mothers from the irrational emotions that increase fear and pain. However if pain-free and fear-free birth defines success, most men are destined for failure...Pain-free and fear-free is an ideal, not a standard by which to judge success."[54] As for the inclusion of fathers into the alternative birthing revolution, Bradley had the most to say, with LeBoyer having the least input.

Reed also goes on to say, "Despite the ideological similarities of three childbirth reformers - Dick-Read, Lamaze, and Bradley - there are significant differences in their proposals. Driven by their pragmatic interest in birthing babies rather than any theoretical coherence, they advocate distinct programs and practices. Most important, the three birth models emphasize different aspects of mothers' experience and fathers' involvement: Dick-Read recognizes the magic of the event; Lamaze, the power of mothers to train their bodies; and Bradley, the importance of fathers' role."[55]

Since the early 1980s and up until today, there have been, and are still, a whole host of books that claim to be new birthing methods, and others that are tweaks on some of the original five. Here are a few examples.

---

[54] Reed, *Birthing Fathers: The Transformation of Men in American Rites of Birth,* 219
[55] Reed, *Birthing Fathers: The Transformation of Men in American Rites of Birth,* 108

Active Birth: The New Approach to Giving Birth Naturally, by Janet Balaskas, (1992). This author states her philosophy with this paragraph:

> "An active birth is nothing new. It is simply a convenient way of describing normal labor and birth and the way that a woman behaves when she is following her own instincts and the physiological logic of her body. It is a way of saying that she herself controls her body while giving birth, rather than being the passive recipient of a birth that is managed by her attendants."[56]

Of the many birth methods that I've read, this one seems to be the most pro-home birth. I found very few references to husbands or fathers and the illustrations even have other women helping the mother. Towards the end of the book, I did find one resource for the birth partner. There is a small section at the very end titled "Emergency Birth: For the Partner". It states: "If you are alone with a woman who is about to give birth and are unable to reach a midwife or doctor." What follows are two pages of very brief instructions of how to take care of the laboring woman until a midwife or a doctor arrives. I think most fathers will get the hint on this one.

One of the more popular authors who challenged traditional hospital policies was Ina May Gaskin with her book *Spiritual Midwifery* (1975). I discovered that her book is around 45% birth stories, 45% medical terminology related to the pregnancy, and 10% musings with a vague philosophical bent, sometimes including anti-medical institutional statements. There is not much material directed at fathers' roles, beyond the standard pregnancy information.

Rose St. John wrote a book aimed specifically at fathers titled *Fathers at Birth* (2009). Her perspective is to instruct the father to become a 'mountain and a warrior'. The mountain aspect is to help the mother remain calm, and the warrior aspect is to defend her

---

[56] Balaskas, Janet, *Active Birth: The New Approach to Giving Birth Naturally,* (Harvard: The Harvard Common Press, 1992), 1.

from unnecessary intrusions while she is peacefully laboring. The message is good, but the language is very New-Agey at times.

Another book directed at fathers is *The Birth Partner, a Complete Guide to Childbirth for Dads, Doulas, and All Other Labor Companions* (2008). Like most books, the focus here is on the medical aspects of pregnancy, with additional focus on breathing and relaxation techniques for labor. I think this is a decent book for fathers who want to be well informed medically and also want to be well prepared.

I wanted to include Sheila Stubbs' book for its unique approach to traditional birthing method books and guides. There is a difference between a short birth story, and a week by week guide of what is occurring biologically during pregnancy. Sheila Stubbs' book *Birthing the Easy Way* (2005) is a good example of something in between the hard right and soft left ways of discussing and introducing birth. It does not have many resources for fathers, but it does give a good look inside what a real mother might actually be thinking during her journey through many births.

The last birth method that I came across in my research was the McMoyler Method. From what I can gather, this is a very new start up, and most of its resources are located online at http://mcmoylermethod.com/index.html. The website seems to be more focused on classes and instruction than the open and interactive dialogue that usually accompany other websites in today's internet culture. The class content appears to be based on the usual medical and relaxation aspects of birth.

I mentioned the *Fathers-To-Be Handbook* briefly in the chapter dealing with internet resources. The book itself is by Patrick M. Houser (2007), whose wife had the first documented water birth in the United States. If I had to pick a book that had the most overpowering mix of birth stories and new age terminology, this would be it. There is a useful section at the end with links and resources for fathers on all aspects of birth.

I have spoken many times about the choices of where mothers may wish to labor. To recap, there is the traditional hospital setting, home birth, and what I call third party locales.

Examples of these can be birthing centers and outdoor or nature settings. There is a book out there for fathers whose partners chose to homebirth. Leah Hazard's *The Fathers Homebirth Handbook* (2008), is definitely unique. Even though the book has birth stories, the rest of the format is not the textbook medical approach that many other birth books out there center on. Its main format is answering common questions that many fathers ask about home births. To say the least, it was a refreshing read on a type of birth largely neglected by many birth authors.

The most comprehensive guide for fathers is Sheila Kitzinger's *The Complete Book of Pregnancy and Childbirth*. This is a massive book, but every chapter is well worth the reading. It does include the large amount of medical information that most pregnancy and birth books discuss, but it differs in many other aspects. The tone throughout the book is always directed at both parents, which is a feat in and of itself. However, in addition to the biological approach, she includes discussions for many other aspects of the birth. She offers emotional advice and fascinating anecdotes that can actually help the father help the laboring mother have a very well rounded and healthy birth, regardless of location.

There are many birth and pregnancy guides directed at fathers, but just as there are good books, there are some that are bad. It may be a harsh statement, but it is only my opinion. Some of these examples are: *The Guy's Guide to Surviving Pregnancy, Childbirth, and the First Year of Fatherhood* by Michael Crider, *The Dude's Guide to Pregnancy: Dealing With Your Expecting Wife, Coming Baby, and the End of Life as You Knew It* by Bill Lloyd and Scott Finch, *She's Having a Baby - and I'm Having a Breakdown* by James Douglas Barron, *The New Dad's Survival Guide* by Scott Mactavish, *The Caveman's Pregnancy Companion: a Survival Guide for Expectant Fathers* by David Port and John Ralston, *My Boys Can Swim! The Official Guy's Guide to Pregnancy* by Ian Davis, and *How Men Have Babies: The Pregnant Father's Survival Guide* by Alan Thicke.

After the guides come the books with only birth stories. These are very easy to find, but the one that stuck out most to me was one that was written in 1985. It offers a unique glimpse into a time period that is not as well documented as today. The book is *Fathers: There At The Birth*, by Tim Spacek. Even though the book is almost all birth stories by other fathers, the author does state that his intention is to re-open dialogues and make the discussion of birth a normal activity among fathers. I agree wholeheartedly with his efforts.

Lastly, we come to the history books. The two powerhouses on the subject of fathers and birth are Richard K. Reed and Judith Walzer Leavitt.

Leavitt's book, *Make Room for Daddy: The Journey From Waiting Room to Birthing Room*, is a good modern history book, and many of her areas of research run parallel to Reed. She focuses on a very specific time frame, 1935 to 1985. Her book is a fun read for lots of little historical footnotes that you don't normally read about in birth books and guides. Leavitt gives a tad more credit to the late 1800s OB and goes back a little further in history than Reed, where Reed goes more in depth to the present. There is only one flaw in both her and Reed's approach, which is that they spend too much time highlighting the problem of the lack of roles for fathers. They tread very lightly in offering the very first steps to finding solutions.

Reed's book, *Birthing Fathers: The Transformation of Men in American Rites of Birth*, is the best source I found for explaining and breaking down the medical model, the philosophy used in almost all hospitals. He also dedicates a considerable amount of pages to the subjects of birth classes and couvade. I did not find a better research attempt at all of the philosophies and ideas that make developing roles for fathers very difficult. Reed and Leavitt don't just delve into history; they also make a case for the further development of roles for fathers at birth.

Top Picks

It goes without saying that of all the books I found on the topic of fathers and birth, I had favorites. There were also some that I did not like at all. These are not criticisms of the authors themselves, just an opinion of their books on the strict context of usefulness for fathers who wish to find resources for the development of roles. Their books may be useful in other ways even if I did not like them for role development. The ones that were my favorites were so for the obvious reasons that they gave me lots of resources and research that helped with the shaping of this book.

I'll get my least favorites out of the way first. Alan Thicke's book, *How Men Have Babies* struck a nerve with me. While money is rightfully a concern during pregnancy, it should not be the primary and overwhelming concern. It is quite annoying to read a rich white celebrity complain about how expensive children's things are that most middle class fathers out there would never dream of purchasing.

Ian Davis' book *My Boys Can Swim!* had the same financial overtone as Thicke's, but he also wrote in a tone that spoke of the whole pregnancy affair as one big nuisance. Thicke and Davis both apparently wrote books that were half complaints and half rants. They then tried to pass them under the guise of humor, which is the worst kind of pandering out there.

Lastly, is the book *Your Pregnancy, For the Father-To-Be*, by Glade B. Curtis and Judith Schuler. These authors wrote a series of books about pregnancy and included one for fathers. Let me say first, that I am not anti-hospital. I am against not giving people chances to express their individuality and uniqueness. Almost all birth books out there, good and bad, take the stance that each birth is different and no two couples are the same. While this book did cover the basics about the medical side of birth, there was no book worse than this one in that it basically tells fathers to go to a hospital, sit in a corner, and let the important people do the real work. This book is the king of the 'how to be a good and passive patient' books out there and it is directed right at the father. Read it with caution; not only is it not a good resource for developing better roles for fathers, it actually indirectly takes away any power to develop a role to begin with.

My favorite three books were by Richard K. Reed, Armin Brott, and Sheila Kitzinger. Sheila Kitzinger's book is the one book I would recommend to fathers if they wanted to know everything they could about pregnancy and wanted to find it in one place. Where my book is more of a primer on how to pick and choose what information is out there, *The Complete Guide to Pregnancy and Childbirth* is the best information and preparation book out there for couples, in my opinion.

However, if a father wants an information and preparation book for fathers only, Armin Brott's book, *The Expectant Father: Facts, Tips, and Advice for Dads-To-Be,* is top notch. His writing style does overwhelm the reader with pandering, but it also doesn't go too much into the technical and medical side of the issue. Straightforward and practical is the best way to describe his writing style.

Pregnancy information and preparation aside, Richard Reed's book *Birthing Fathers* deals specifically with the roles and functions that have been and are available to fathers. This author also presents the best possible solutions to breaking down the stereotypes that the traditional birth method places most fathers into. Any father who reads this book will feel well informed, and armed and ready to start down the path of making himself more useful for his wife's birth.

The books that I read but did not feel the need to review here are listed in the bibliography.

Is this part where I casually put on my sunglasses?

After reading lots of books just so that I could pick them apart for useful information, which could be assembled for developing new roles, I came across a few quandaries. There are four main circumstances that present the biggest challenges facing fathers who wish to find role development resources in books relating to birth.

1: Pandering. Almost all of the books written for fathers by fathers had some level of pandering in them. Even Armin Brott had a few too many cartoons scattered throughout his book. The titles alone of a lot of the books I listed should give the first clue of how bad some of these books pander. The assumption that a book for fathers about pregnancy and birth must be funny or the father won't read it has many negative ramifications. It insults the intelligence.

There is a huge difference between putting in one or two jokes or cartoons to help lighten the mood and not overwhelm some of the more casual fathers, and writing the whole book in the theme that men are idiots and its layout is that of the Sunday comics.

Birth books for fathers don't have to be written in pure medical and biological terminology, but they also don't have to be written for sixteen year old boys. That was why Armin Brott's book made my top three; he was one of the very few authors that found that middle ground of writing that appealed to fathers from all walks of life. Pandering assumes the lowest common denominator of an audience, that men don't really care and humor makes it bearable, and at worst, that's how men should act during the pregnancy and labor. If someone wants to read a humorous book about pregnancy and kids that doesn't pander, then I suggest *Fatherhood* by Bill Cosby.

2: The 9-3-2 Observation. I noticed that most pregnancy and birth books fell into an obvious pattern. I am not saying that this pattern is wrong, but that fathers seeking books about birth specifically should just be aware of it. 9-3-2 books spend most of their time talking about the 9 months of pregnancy, the 3 stages of labor, and a varying time frame after the birth of 2 days, 2 weeks, or 2 years. It is also a pattern than most 9-3-2 books deal with the "3" part in an extremely brief period. I learned the hard way that when reading these books for the examination of fathers at the birth itself, I had to slog through the same 9 month pregnancy information that was in almost all the other 9-3-2 books. That is also why I recommended Sheila Kitzinger's *Complete Guide to Pregnancy and Childbirth*, it should be the only 9-3-2 book the fathers should have to read. On a side note, the best "2 Year" book is *Fatherhood, An Anthology*, edited by John Lewis Stempel. In this book, the editor compiles quotes from fathers throughout all places in history for a good idea of how great men from all cultures have seen little tidbits of fatherhood.

Once a father gets past the 9-3-2 trap, he can start looking for books that deal only with the "3" stage, the 3 stages of labor. There are few. Bradley's *Husband Coached Childbirth*, Reed's *Birthing*

Fathers, Hazard's *Home Birth Handbook*, and a few of the short pandering guides were all I found. There is not much to work with. To gather resources for developing new roles, one can either flip to certain points in the 9-3-2 books, concentrate on the short selection of books about the actual birth for fathers, or do both. For my book, I did both, so that no other fathers had to. My book's only "2" covers the 2 weeks after birth so that the father can be aware of and possibly prevent the different forms of postpartum conditions and know when expert help might be needed.

3: Publication Cycle: The next logical conclusion that the existence of so many pandering books, yet so few serious books about men and the actual birth brings us to, is that this field of publishing is not important. Basically, publishers do not print more books like Brott's because they think no one is interested or it is not important. On the flip side, fathers are not interested and may not think it is important because there are not more books on the subject. It is a frustrating conundrum for those fathers looking for materials to develop their own stance to assist their wife in the choosing and execution of a birth plan. This cycle also prevents the development of modern resources for fathers.

If a father goes to a regular bookstore, a used bookstore, or online bookstore even, it is very hard to find their resources. Most of the ones that he may find border on comic books. There is very little variety out there. Not only is that a direct problem, but it gives the indirect impression to large publishers that different types of books should either not be published, or that they should follow the basic 9-3-2 format. This circumstance has the horrible effect of keeping expectant fathers both ignorant and apathetic to the upcoming birth.

4: The Birthing Logic Quagmire. As a result of the alternative birthing movement, led by what I call the Five Benevolent Technocrats, (Dick-Read, Bradley, Lamaze, LeBoyer, and Odent) we arrive at the Logical Birth Quagmire. The original birth methods created by these authors were supposed to put the power back into the hands of the mothers, but since they adhered to the traditional hospital's medical model and setting, in the end it actually took more power away from them. The medical model, to paraphrase Reed, now has fathers as managers, defenders, and representatives. It follows then, that any birth method or approach that uses those three terms defends and reinforces the medical model, even if it's not aware of it. This is the Birthing Logic Quagmire. Hospitals are somewhat aware of this reinforcement but many other authors are not, even some who want to challenge the medical model.

The Benevolent Technocrats had good intentions. They simply did not, could not, or would not take the step to think outside of the hospital. Therefore, the hospitals turned their teachings into a technocracy that supported its own biomedical institution, as defined by Reed. They did not start out as technocrats on purpose, but they let the hospital administrations turn them into such by turning their movements against themselves, which in the end, hindered women from having the birth they wanted, and even further, the roles that fathers want at those births.

I must put in disclaimer here however. Some the books discussed here are old, and may be obsolete. Some of these writers may still be writing or their views may have changed. What matters is that their books did inspire movements that are based on the ideas presented originally. Analyzing the book that initiated a movement is the point of the reviews; not to paint the author in only one light or color. Yes, there is a Technocracy, but only in its influence and not the personal identities.

To use an example, at first the term and definition of coach had impact, in its time. Ever since the medical model adopted it, it has been re-defined as a passive and impotent hospital role. The hospital father as coach is trained to do as little as possible to be technically involved, but still in the position to be pushed aside and overridden when any real choices are to be made.

How do you know so much about models?

Our last discussion brings us to birthing classes. Once again, Richard K. Reed has the best summary of what these classes are about, "What are the meta messages of birthing classes? Not surprisingly, they are as conflicted as the childbirth theories from which they derive. The alternative birthing movement was demanded by parents who sought control over birth; it was developed by obstetricians who were embedded in a biological model; and it has been institutionalized in hospitals that empower physicians and technicians. Birthing education becomes an arena for the negotiation of discourse about the meaning of birth. Holistic birthers, physicians, childbirth agencies, and hospitals all seek to control how couples become educated for birth. The result has been dissonance between the ideals of the childbirth movement and the realities of birthing in hospitals. Couples are taught that the ideal birth is without pain or medication, yet birthing classes warn them to expect both. They are taught to make informed decisions, and yet are to unquestioningly obey the decrees of their physician. They learn to defend themselves from the interventions of Medical Technology, but hear that they need the hospital for safety and support."[57] It is plain to see that most birth classes hinder true role development for both fathers and mothers.

My Roles

Anyone who tells a man that they want to empower him so that he can participate in a birth, or uses any other such language, is wasting their breath. If someone was to tell a man that they were giving him the materials so that he could make an informed choice – they would get a much more serious response. Add to that, if he decided he didn't want to participate in a birth, (regardless of location, attendants, or circumstances), even after being given the correct information, i.e., not based on negative stereotypes and demeaning attitudes, at least he could give rational or logical reasons for his choosing to do so. That is what this book is attempting to do.

My suggested roles must break the four cycles presented in this chapter. They must let the father express himself, let him have a subjective and personal experience of the entire pregnancy and birth - while at the same time supporting the mother in the exact same way for the same reasons and goals. Birth is not only biological and logical. It is everything that is cultural. Roles must be designed to

---

[57] Reed, *Birthing Fathers: The Transformation of Men in American Rites of Birth,* 137

represent the many different aspects of culture: social, spiritual, religious, emotional, etc. I don't think there is one golden role that can fulfill all these aspects, so I created more than one to try to focus on them all at different levels.

The goal of this book is to present roles that do not just reach out to the average person, but appeal to the common sense in everyone.

Chapter Nine
Roles

When it comes to the role of the father, the very first step to birth begins when the mother chooses what type of birth she wants. She has a very large field of options to consider, like where, when, how, and with who. The next step is for the father to choose or develop the role that would both best suit his personality type and also be useful to the mother and the type of birth she has chosen. The last step is that both parents tweak and develop both their choices to fit their chosen birth plan.

The key to the creation of a role is to put the birth in certain context. Pregnancy and birth can be seen as a story. There may be a few plot twists, but we are all pretty sure of the few ways that this story will end. The parents are the characters in this somewhat predictable plot. Knowing that, there is no reason that every person can't create their own unique personality to operate within the storyline of childbirth. The example roles I created are simply characters in this well-known story.

The point of these roles varies: to use these unique styles to absorb and apply the 9-3-2 medical information, to set the stage where the birth partner can be supportive to the mother in all ways, emotional, mental, physical, etc., and at the same time, giving room for his needs to be addressed, expressed, communicated, and put out in the open. Specific events and actions are listed, but are used as examples, not strict instructions.

I created these examples by studying the many birth stories by dads, the manner and tone of the books directed at fathers, and observation of general personality types. These character sketches can be funny, but the point is not to entertain, it is to present options and ways that fathers would want to be involved. As we learned earlier about the barrier of overwhelming medical knowledge, it is nearly impossible to know all of the pertinent information. If the birth partner is comfortable and confident, then any new information is processed better. It will be much easier for fathers to stay relaxed, to avoid tension or anxiety, and to make better choices in the midst of any new or unplanned for situations by adapting one of my example roles.

It is not meant for fathers to try to fit neatly into these examples. The goal is to recognize them, to build upon them, to fix them, to make them better, to develop them, to mix and match them to unique mothers and situations. These are the building blocks of new and better defined efforts. These roles are not set in stone, they are set up as bare bones personality descriptions that are designed to be altered or added to. They are not meant to be strictly adhered to literally, but followed more in the spirit of the meaning.

I did take the mothers' needs and the desires of fathers' into account directly. I started with fathers' needs first, so that they may feel useful. The hoped-for effect is that the mother won't need to worry about her partner throughout the pregnancy and during the birth, and she may also tweak and change the proposed roles to better accommodate her wishes. That seems to be the easiest process. Richard Reed can describe this part of the process much better than I: "As the mother pulls inward to her inner resources of birth, the father seems to rely increasingly on core aspects of his relationship with his partner. What role do they play for each other? How do they work to solve other kinds of problems? This relationship offers direction to the most effective strategy to help, be that coaching, holding her hand, or just observing. The exigencies of birthing strip away the complexities of intention and planning, leaving most fathers with the strategies that they have developed elsewhere in their relationship. Several dads who felt successful about coaching their wives through transition referred directly back to their relationship. Martin reported, 'I guess I've always been the one who took control when things got tough, and it sure got tough there for a while.'"[58]

---

[58] Reed, *Birthing Fathers: The Transformation of Men in American Rites of Birth,* 191.

Some roles may have a physical symbol: the binder, a clipboard, bag of sacred items. Most of the roles will also have at least one Evil Twin, which is what can happen if the role turns into a negative stereotype. These twins are what happens when the birth partner goes overboard, or what each role could turn into without the self-awareness and a primary concern for the mother. Each role will have a more artistic overview, a brief introduction, so that the mother can also be aware of which attitudes the father is developing.

I spent a lot of time considering whether or not to create a role specifically for a woman birth partner, a sister, lover, mother, or friend who is not a midwife, doula, or any other type of medical professional. I decided against it. I wish to target and bring into the fold fathers first. However, I will outline the process in its entirety and I sincerely hope that these roles can be adapted to any type of birth partners and that furthermore, with my resources and structures, new ones can be created specifically for any personality or circumstance.

The key for mothers to accept these roles is that the fathers are emotionally present and supportive.

Here are some tips to the process. In the print chapter, I discussed the 9-3-2 time frame format that most birth books use. For a quick review, here is the terminology:

- The "9" section, meaning discussions about the pregnancy up to the birth
- The "3" stages of birth
- The "2" chapter, which I mean by the first two weeks of life, while most others mean the first two months or years.

The Landmarks and the Choices lists are samples of what to ask yourself and the mother when choosing or developing a role. All of my landmark approaches should be taken into consideration for roughly 30% pregnancy, 70% labor and birth. For the 30% part, the focus is the development of methods for communication, emotional health, financial concerns, medical understanding, and stress management. For the 70% part, do not stay stuck in the 9-3-2 mentality. The goal is to develop and examine the "3" part of the equation, without getting bogged down into minutia. Remember, you're creating a character, these are his motivations.

Here are some scenarios I used to create the example roles for birth partners. The first one is for the 30% of the actions and functions that the birth partner will develop for his role. These are more in the spirit of starting a character creation for the story of the birth.

Questions for the father to ask himself: How will he participate or react to these occasions?

6-8 weeks:
• The Announcement
• The First Symptoms

3rd month:
• First Prenatal appointment
• The mother has probably chosen the type of birth (if not chosen beforehand, but officially now with medical appointments)
• May hear the heartbeat
• Couvade could start at anytime

4th Month:
• Brott's Financial Planning advice should be considered
• Risk of miscarriage is greatly reduced
• Buying and reading of books
• Start playing music to the baby

5th Month:
• Gender can be determined
• Shop around for childbirth education classes
• Mental preparations to be made
• Maternity wardrobe bought, if this is her first baby. If not, this may need to happen earlier.

6th Month:
• Nesting may start
• Feel the baby moving
• Plan work leave
• Start birth plan

7th Month:
• Start childbirth classes

- Reading to the baby
- Arrange for extra birth attendants, if desired
- Start checklists

8th Month:
- Name choices
- Registering at birth location, scouting, and setup
- Packing, if not a home birth
- Preparing for all contingencies

9th Month:
- Be ready and waiting

Choices for Role Development

After the mother has chosen the type and location of the birth, these questions are to help *both* parents decide what they want out of the birth. Most of these are for both the mother and father to review, but some are for one or the other. All of these questions are designed to help the parents develop the best role for the birth partner during labor. These choices are for the 70% of the actions and desires during the labor itself. These questions are to help the character reach their full potential during the birth.

- How do you both normally relieve stress?
- How is serious communication established? (Over dinner, during drives, sit downs, music sessions, etc.)
- How much will the birth plan be relied upon and enforced during labor? What type of birth attitude and language will be used?
- Who will do the handling of insurance, and admittance? How soon will you do all the paperwork required, if you do it?
- When will you both tour and scope out the birth location? When will the mother want to start planning for the arrangement of necessities there, such as overnight bag, checklists, spiritual items, books, Wi-Fi, etc?
- Will there be a water birth? Will the pool or tub be rented, built, or provided?
- When will you start the preparations for balancing the work schedule and impending labor: How will you notify coworkers

when it is time? Will the mother be able to contact the father quickly at his work?

- How will you both speak to the baby during pregnancy, if at all?
- Will the father want to choose slings, bottles, cloths, diapers, clothing and carrying preferences that he likes?
- Who will make arrangements and communicate with friends and family, during and after the birth?
- Will there be other children in attendance, and will it depend on the location of the birth?
- Who will wrangle the other attendants, such as family, friends, medical staff, doulas, midwife, etc.?
- Will the father keep track of birth and postural aids: the birth ball, bean bag, pillows, birth stool, etc.?
- How much discussion will there be about understanding and administering pain relief methods?
- How will the father handle the clothing and birth room accessories immediately after birth?
- Will a Masseuse be hired, or will the father start practicing massage methods early on?
- Will you both want to keep the placenta and the cord? If so, for what purpose?
- What will be the father's attitude towards doulas, midwives, nurses, and other staff/attendants?
- Who will wrangle babysitters and family/friends for house-sitting?
- Who will prepare the food and drinks for labor, for the both of you?
- Will the father want to, or be able to administer any type of exam that laymen can perform such as cervix dilation, breathing, and pulse?
- What are the mothers opinions on cesareans, other complications, and medical interventions (needed or not)?
- What relaxation methods will the mother prefer during labor? Examples are music, incense, oils, aromatherapy, yoga, meditation, etc. Which of these will also work for the father?

- Will there be an adult attendant, who has been at a birth, to chaperone any children who wish to attend?
- How do you both want the infant to spend its first 24 hours after birth?
- What is the mothers preferred form of emotional support?
- How will the father monitor distractions like lights, noises, staff, and attendants?
- Is there unique awareness or insight of the stages of labor that would help either parent understand it better, such as acts in a play, stages of a military operation, plays of a game, etc.?
- Will there be any rituals or celebrations for when the baby is brought home? Will they be private or have guests? These can range from quiet spiritual relaxation to a boisterous housewarming.

After reading these sets of questions, the father should have a good idea of what he and mother want out of birth, and what type of character, i.e., role, that he wants to create. The next step is to take those ideas and apply them to the story of birth. To reflect this, I have re-tuned the "3" *medical* stages of birth for the mother to the 5 *laymen* stages of birth for the father. These stages are triggered, or coincide around the three medical stages.

Here are my 5 Laymen Stages of Birth: the **Alpha Stage**, **Stage 1**, **Stage 2**, **Stage 3**, and the **Omega Stage**.

The **Alpha Stage** consists primarily of the finishing of classes, having the books read, completing the checklists, and the finishing touches of all other general preparations of the first 6 months of pregnancy. This stage is completed and the father is ready for Stage 1 when he is at that ready and waiting period.

Stage 1: The baby moves around to get into position. The birth partner can help or let nature take its course. When it comes to cervix dilation, the birth partner can check this as well as medical professionals. A Bishop's score can be taken if labor isn't progressing (for medical staff only, but make sure you are familiar with it). This is a key time for relaxation and getting comfortable. This stage averages around twenty hours. This is when latent labor gives way to active labor. This is a good time for settling in and preparing the birth location.

Stage 2: This starts when the baby is coming down the birth canal and ends when the baby emerges. At this point vocal or non-verbal support must be at its utmost. The cervix is more or less 10 cm. When the baby's head emerges from the vagina is typically when the mother experiences the Ring of Fire. The mother will be bearing down or pushing. This is when the father can catch the baby. It is critical that the father never leave the mother's side during this stage. This is coincidentally the usual time when episiotomies are pushed on the mother. Some small tearing may occur and need not cause concern.

Stage 3: The first landmark of this stage is the birth of the placenta, followed by an emotional release by both the parents. The cord cutting by the father usually follows. Some parents wait for the cord to stop pulsing, or even have a lotus birth. The father may want to assure the immediate physical contact of the mother and baby. This is the favorite time for many fathers for photos and mementos. This stage officially ends when the placenta is delivered.

The **Omega Stage**: This is the time for phone calls and the thanking of attendants – both medical and layperson. Placenta rituals can be done at this time. The pronouncement of the infant's name can take place at this time. The next part of this stage is the Homecoming. After the mother and infant are settled in, the father may watch for BT, PPD, PD, etc. (There is a 70-80% possibility of one of these happening in the two weeks after the birth that is called the Omega Stage.) This means doing everything possible to give the mother as much time and whatever she needs to recover from this huge event - for at least two weeks. This is also the time to connect and bond with the baby yourself, from the moment of birth until the normal routine of life picks up again. Keep an eye out for bills in the mail.

Each father is unique. However, there will be some commonalities throughout all the roles such as physically being there when the baby actually comes out, and an emotional response appropriate to your unique personality.

I thought that giving the role an identity to relate with, beyond mere caricature, would be extremely helpful. Some roles will be proactive; others may be passive for beginners. I must also add that when I named a role after a real person or character, I am not describing their actual personality but rather focusing on certain traits. They inspired me to create these roles. It should also be remembered that some roles are stronger and more involved than others, as personalities differ in levels of assertiveness, we can't all be extremely outgoing. The roles are not to be viewed as pigeonholing or cornering stereotypes meant to limit or hold back fathers. They are platforms of personality traits to build upon, gateway archetypes to be stepped into for the process of creating a unique mold for every individual father.

In essence, you can't fake the birthing hour. It's when we shine. Pregnancy shows us how we are husbands, the birthing hour shows how we will be fathers and husbands. It is about the father being himself. These roles are to serve as examples and guides.

The R. W. Emerson

Ralph Waldo Emerson is a famous poet who wrote about philosophy and spirituality from the 1840s to the 1870s. One of his best known works is an essay called *Nature*. He also wrote and lectured on many other subjects including individuality, the soul, and freedom. What is not well known is that he spent some time early in his life in the church as a pastor.

Emerson was a very spiritual man who left the mainstream channels of religion so that he could create his own worship. While he did not create or advocate any one specific religion over the other, he preferred to seek out the divine in what we today would call mother nature. He saw spirituality in everyday things and had great trust in natural processes. The person who blazes his own trail and searches for the divine in everything is a prime source of inspiration for this role.

This birth partner is highly spiritual but does not have to be associated with adherence to any one religion. He will have the medical and logistical details taken care of early on, so that he can spend the birth focused on the spirituality of the situation. It may be wise for this father to let anyone attending the birth, at any location, know that they may witness unusual rituals and ceremonies such as whispering in the baby's ear at birth or keeping the placenta for planting under a tree. These examples are becoming common and do not necessarily mean that the couple is overtly spiritual, but that sometimes a multitude of uncommon practices can catch some people off-guard.

Symbol: The Icon – a relic, totem, trinket, etc.; for both him and the mother that they will carry throughout the pregnancy and use during the birth as a source of confidence and strength. Examples such as a rosary, a cross, a small statue, an ankh, or a notebook of passages from their favorite holy book such as the Koran, New Testament, Buddhist meditations, transcendentalists sayings, or just random tidbits of wisdom collected over the years.

Alpha Stage

The official announcement of the pregnancy will most likely be public in their place of worship or practice: a temple, church, congregation, mosque, or other such group setting. It could be followed privately by a grand ritual or spiritual celebration.

When the mother experiences the first symptoms, both parents may enjoy quiet solitude and start to make their mental preparations.

During the prenatal appointments, he will be very concerned with the atmosphere. The birthing room must be able to support metaphysical observation and participation. He will want them to be able to take a step back or retreat into personal and sacred space. At the hospital tour, he will make sure she can adhere to any religious or spiritual choices, and possibly the setting up of a table that can serve as a mini altar for spiritual items.

When this father feels the first kick, he may rush off to his quiet space for some intense introspection, and then share his comments or feelings with the mother, also while encouraging her to do the same, and then talking about in depth. He may also do another small celebration ritual.

The methods of stress relief and also the mode of communication for this role will be in the realm of whatever their spiritual or belief system is. Many people can be intensely spiritual without being religious and perhaps even vice-versa. It is not my desire to discuss the how or why of this stance, but only to point out that it is okay for fathers to act and speak in highly spiritual languages and also not be too preachy or dogmatic.

Labor (Stages 1-3)

Meditation is a highly effective form of stress relief for the father and pain management for the mother during labor. In today's more enlightened culture, it is okay for people to embrace meditation without being a Hindu or Buddhist. This is what I mean by being spiritual without being religious, and also may only be one of the spiritual resources used. It would be very easy to mesh breathing styles originally developed for birth alongside established meditations.

This father will read any books given to him by the mother, as well as ones he has chosen for their spiritual and philosophical outlook on the entire birthing process. He may even study rituals and beliefs from indigenous cultures from around the globe for tips and epiphanies. The medical approach may not be the first thing he thinks of during labor, but he will certainly know enough to keep up with others if there are medical attendants, or if at home. He will be aware of the specific parts of the stages the mother is going through. He will keep his head wrapped around the lists, and will most likely have one major checklist kept with the icons.

If not chosen already long before the official pregnancy, he will put a great amount of thought into the choice of his icon that will accompany him throughout the labor. He will also spend a great deal of effort making sure that the mother has her perfect icon that she will readily be able to connect with for strength and confidence during labor.

Sheila Kitzinger gives a great example of a spiritual icon in her book: "In some Mediterranean cultures, women have a flower beside them when they are in labor. It is the rose of Jericho, which looks dried up and lifeless but in the heat of the birth room opens and spreads its petals wide. In southern Italy they call it 'the hand of the Mother of God'. It is both a symbol of the help that Mary gives them in childbirth and of the cervix that is opening wider and wider so that the baby can be born. In Mediterranean cultures, too, there is a tradition of ritual actions that provide a powerful sense for the woman in labor of everything being opened and released, so that she can feel her body opening in a similar way. In Greece, grain or water may be poured, windows and doors flung wide, and clothing unbuttoned."[59]

---

[59] Kitzinger,Sheila. *The Complete Book of Pregnancy and Childbirth.* 4th ed. (New York: Alfred A. Knopf, 2005), 204.

Omega Stage

The father may give the infant a ritual bath when born (when the mother decides the infant is ready). At home, he may create special sacred space and sanctity in which the mother can recover. Muslim fathers try to ensure that the first taste of the newborn is sweet and will put honey in their mouths while whispering their faith's call to prayer in their ear.

Evil Twin

The Chanting Monk: he may get so wrapped up in maintaining a relaxed and spiritual environment that he will forget about the laboring mother, and may detach himself from the situation and become distant and not helpful.

The FDR

Franklin Delano Roosevelt was the 32nd United States president who served from 1933-1945. He was the American leader during the Second World War and is considered by many to be one of the greatest presidents in American history. He died of a stroke before the end of his last term in office. The list of his many amazing accomplishments during his time as president would be too large to present here.

What makes this president unique for our purposes is that he was the first to harness a technological innovation. During his terms in office he was the first president to use radio in a unique way to connect with the American public. Using fireside chats, FDR was able to connect more closely with the people to describe the inner workings of his policies. A more modern description would be that of a digital or technological storyteller. It is important to remember that Roosevelt was a leader first, storyteller second.

Even though the connection between FDR and modern technology is not apparent at first - this role is an evolution from the stereotypical camera dad of the 1980s. However, thanks in part to today's extensive social media outlets that go far beyond the capabilities of radio, this father will have up to date, minute by minute details for friends and family via all these new forms of multimedia. He wants to make sure that everyone can have access to the mother's emotional and medical conditions, in real time. A clever mother can manipulate this dad into checking her birthing checklists while checking his own media checklists.

Where the old version would have a video camera as well as a regular one, today's father can turn the whole event into a live action media frenzy. This is not say that he will invade the laboring mother's privacy, but this could be in reaction to her having many friends and family who aren't actually at the birth, but want to stay very informed and up to date. The camera dad of the last generation did not have the huge variety of social media that we have now at our disposal.

For the film aspect, he may to visit the birthing location prior to the event to check acoustics and lighting. He may buy a premium camera (if he doesn't own one already) and perhaps even an external microphone. Some may even go so far as to interview the people involved before and after, on camera. For the social media outlets, you can be damn sure the delivery room better have Wi-Fi.

Being an FDR does not mean ignoring the mother in a time of need to get a good shot, or a status update. It means that he will express his care and involvement through a powerful collection of videos, photos, and scrapbooks to be enjoyed long after the birth, and perhaps even for grandkids. He will still do the basics, such as following the birth plan, backing up her choices, keeping her calm, hydrated, and relaxed, etc.

Symbol: The Tablet; or the laptop, smartphone - any electronic gadget that will let him interface and monitor all his media outlets. It will be like an electronic birth binder.

Alpha Stage

When the mother finds out that she is pregnant, it will put a great strain on this dad to let her friends and family know privately before everyone on the planet knows through his social media outlets. I would like to think that there will be times during pregnancy when he realizes that the mother just needs quiet intimacy from him, like when the baby moves, and that he can have plenty of time afterwards to talk about it to whomever he wants.

This father will supplement the birthing classes by using resources from the Internet. He may watch online videos, read forums for tips, and email buddies who have children for advice. During the tour of the birthing location, he may pick out a corner in which to put his desk. That desk will have space for his tablet, laptop, camera, etc.

Communication with the mother during pregnancy and labor should not be an issue for this father as he lives for telling the story. Stress management, on the other hand, might be the most difficult for this father, as he may keep himself and his wife on a high public profile during pregnancy. My first suggestion would be finding times to unplug with his wife. This would mean taking time away from the world, friends and family, to have some quiet, private time.

Labor (Stages 1-3)

Labor is tricky for this father. He will have to develop a keen sense of his wife's on-the-spot needs to determine whether she wants him helping her with or without the electronics at his side. It is not easy to slip away to let her friends know how she is doing. The camera will most likely be static, set up in a corner, as no one does the in-your-face style of filming that was shown in the movie *Nine Months*. The flip side is that he may be lucky enough to be able to receive suggestions from the wife's friends and other mothers by online communication.

The key for this role is finding a way for his newscaster attitude and addiction to online social media to help his wife stay relaxed and focused during labor. This would seem almost counterintuitive. Perhaps the mother can rest assured that if everything is being recorded and updated, and they are at a hostile birth environment - all that documentation may keep unproductive people at arm's length from her, thus enabling her to have a more relaxed birth.

The mother may also take solace in the fact that many people care about her welfare during labor and want to stay updated. It might give her a warm feeling to know that when all is said and done, there is plenty of material to show others and reminisce about in the many years to come.

Omega Stage

Post Production: this means making sure that all the loose ends are tied up. The actors and movie crew (mother and baby) need plenty of downtime and rest to absorb and review the movie project they just finished. He can spend many of the hours editing, copying, saving files, writing, etc., while holding the baby and letting the mother sleep.

Evil Twin

The Laptop Dad: I read about this type of father in a British article about dads at birth. It basically described this one father who stayed in the corner glued to his laptop the entire time his wife was in labor. I would think that he was not very helpful.

The Jean-Baptiste Lully

Jean Baptiste Lully lived from 1632 to 1687. He was technically born an Italian, but spent most of his life in France and promoting its music and culture. At a young age, he had great skill with dancing and playing the violin. He wrote many symphonies and operas for the court of King Louis XIV. Lully could feel both the music and the movements that should accompany it. He commanded the stages and concert halls with evenings of music and dancing. He liked tempos and styles of all types.

During my reading about the stages of labor, I kept coming across different and varying lists of birth positions and laboring movements. All the books I read by women stressed the factor of position and movement intently. I was amazed at the sheer variety. I decided to break this type of thinking into time periods. There are movements that can help the mother and baby during pregnancy. Then, there are movements that can relax the mother and help the 1st stage of labor along. After that are movements that can help during the pushing stage, and lastly, there are different positions and movements that a mother can use for when the baby actually emerges.

This role is for the father who is very physically oriented, he may even be a dancer or physical therapist, and wishes to support his wife through the seemingly limitless options of pregnancy and labor movements available. This role may sound more simple and easy than some of the others, but it may be more time consuming. Case and point – some of the movements and dances could turn into exercises and massages.

I must also add another disclaimer – there are times during labor and birth when the mother will want to sit still or be in a non-moving position. This role does not imply that the mother *has* to be moving at all times. When she does want to move, there is a lot the father can help with.

Symbol: The Music Player: any type of music player. For some, it is hard to dance without some good music. Many mothers wish to have music during labor anyway, so it would work out well.

Since this is the digital age, that music player could be his phone, an actual stereo, a CD player, an MP3 player, etc.

Alpha Stage

This father will spend much of the pregnancy researching and practicing the multiple movements that will help the mother with pregnancy, labor, birth pain and relaxation. I recommend *Natural Childbirth the Bradley Way* for a good breakdown of when and how movement helps a pregnant and laboring mother. The father should not stop at just that book, as there are many others with lots of variety to choose from. Sheila Kitzinger talks about the birth orgasm in *The Complete Book of Childbirth and Pregnancy*.

Labor (Stages 1-3)

For the 1st stage of labor, there are positions and movements that can help with pain relief and progression of labor. Here are a few of the many examples: The mother may want to walk with you beside her. She may want to stand face to face with you, with her arms over your shoulders, with her hips swaying. She may want to semi sit or squat with her hips or pelvis swaying. There is a lot of creativity that can be applied to this part of the labor; any type of movement that helps the mother feel better also helps the baby progress. There is room for some creative dancing.

For the 2nd stage of labor, during the birth itself, there are a variety of positions chosen by many different women for pain relief and easing the baby's birth. Here are a few examples: The mother may want the father to hold her up from behind while she is in a squatting position. She may be in an all-fours position, but with her arms over the father's shoulders. He may also hold her up from the front while she squats. She may prefer to stand or kneel over something, a stool, the father, or a bed. There will be movement during this part as well, as contractions aren't known for keeping a mother still.

Omega Stage

The dancing and swaying doesn't end after birth. I can't think of how many ways it would be helpful for the father to rock, sway, coo, and dance with his infant while the mother recuperates. The baby would also benefit from the bonding.

Evil Twin

The Obligatory White-Man-Can't-Dancer: The title pretty much says it all. Don't commit to this role if you don't want to put 100% into the dancing part.

The Sir Charles Berkeley

In the bureaucracy of English Parliament there is a group called the Board of the Green Cloth. One of the many purposes of this committee was to audit the spending accounts of the Royal House. A member of this board was the Comptroller of the Household, and part of their job was to enforce the proper conduct of handling and spending money. There are records of names of people who have held the title of Comptroller going back to at least the 1400s.

Sir Charles Berkeley served on the Board of the Green Cloth as the Comptroller from 1660 to 1662. An important note is that the majority of Americans reading the above entry could not help but notice the similarity to a famous basketball player who had the nickname Sir Charles Barkley.

The man from the 1600s was a royal accountant, the other an athlete. I had a long list of accountants that I had to choose from; I decided to pick one that both American and English readers could recognize. This role is about being more than just an accountant. It is about record keeping for a much higher purpose, while maintaining a presence like a famous athlete.

The Sir Charles Berkeley role is best for the mother who chooses to be alone during birth, which some studies show to be around 10% of mothers. Therefore, his function is to passively create, much more than a stage manager would, a healthy atmosphere for the mother to deliver. He will have taken care of everything possible beforehand, and even afterwards. This father must keep in mind that the mother may change her mind and want him with her during delivery. In that case, he should have another backup role planned.

Symbol: The Pen. Not just any pen, a very expensive pen. His favorite pen. His symbol of power, readiness, and authority.

Alpha Stage

This father will read everything given to him, and then some on his own. Unfortunately, his knowledge will be mostly theoretical and test-worthy. He will be extremely helpful in the research and creating of the birth plan. This father readily explains everything to everyone who asks what will happen with the type of birth planned. He will save the mother a ton of stress in the time leading up to the birth and should not have a problem with communication. He will do the checklists successfully for the mother in the months leading to the event. He will make sure that the wife has all the book and class materials handy to become the master of her birth.

A good example of showing support while maintaining paperwork is an Early Labor Record. The father can make a chart where he can write the time of the contractions, the duration, the time between them, and any other observations that may be useful to the midwife, doula, or doctor when the time comes. There are also several apps out there that serve the same function.

Labor (Stages 1-3)

During the birth, he usually is the hand-holder and communicator to people attending the birth. It might seem like he is just along for the ride, but he is following her cues very closely. The birth plan will be followed. Along with observation and the usual emotional support that he can give while being next to the mother, he will be very aware of all that is happening.

Omega Stage

This father will know when it's also time to put down the paperwork and make sure all arrangements around the house are taken care of. All the bills will be taken care of, leaving him plenty of time to care for and bond with the baby when the mother wants recovery time. Perhaps this father can woo and calm-talk his baby talking about the awesome college trust fund he just set up in their name.

Evil Twins

The Bank Teller: While being a bank teller in its own right is not a bad thing, it would probably be unwise to have that same attitude during pregnancy and labor. What is meant by that is - don't file something and then forget about that person, the mother, the next day; and go on about your other business.

The Assistant Football Coach: This is the guy that will sit on the sidelines and quietly watch and write down everything important that happens - while not actually engaging anyone unless directly told to.

The Euripides

Of all the ancient Greek plays that survived to the modern day, we have the most from Euripides. He lived from 480 to 406 BCE, at about the same time period as Socrates. This playwright lived during a time when the Greek tragedies were becoming more complex relative to the dithyrambs that helped give birth to theater as we think of it today. Compared to the other major playwrights of his time, Aeschylus and Sophocles, Euripides is considered the most innovative.

The way that the tragedies were created and readied for the performance is a bit different than how most people consider plays to be produced today. A few playwrights were selected for a theatrical competition, and each one was funded by one of the city's rich patrons. Once selected, the author wrote, directed, choreographed, and managed the entire event. What is today separated into the separate functions of director, stage manager, producer, etc.; were all done by one person in ancient Greece. In regard to personalities for birth, I view Euripides as one of the more powerful type of stage managers in history.

It takes both the actors and the crew for a performance to be accomplished perfectly in a theater. The stage manager is in charge of both. I believe that a father who takes this approach will be more than prepared and to have an extremely helpful effect on the mother. He must be careful though, as this path is difficult for men who have issues with control. Some things must be delegated or left out.

This father will spend the pregnancy going over the script with the mother. He will prepare his cue book with notes for how the birth is supposed to go, also including the birth plan. He will prepare for any interruptions. He has decided early on as to how much control he will keep, and how much he will delegate to other crew members, i.e., birth attendants.

He will practice perfect control over all the external and internal matters concerning the birth plan. He will plan most of the details and logistics. He is the type of person who enjoys rehearsal dinners for weddings. It is not necessary that he have any actual theater experience.

This role is one of the better ones suited for home or third-party locale births. In this context the mother can be considered the director, or perhaps the main character.

Symbol: The Stage Manager's Handbook. This will contain: names, numbers, emergency back up plans, the birth plan, known allergies, etc. This will be his go to binder for information, choices, and back-up plans.

Alpha Stage

This father isn't so much about the reading, but the practice. He will read a few books, though he will spend much more time putting together his stage manager's book. He will also probably be much more into the classes than most husbands, as it will provide him ample opportunity to visualize the birth and will treat them like rehearsals. Some pregnancy books I read suggested that the mother and father practice labor beforehand - positions and breathing, etc. When the final month comes, this father will prefer to have his binder ready with everything he feels he needs to know. He will have done a few run-throughs of the birth, and will be ready for the opening night.

Labor (Stages 1-3)

During labor, his binder will most likely just be a reassuring crutch, placed somewhere near where the mother is laboring. He may consult it if a few minor deviations arise, but will have most of it memorized. Since this father really shines while preparing during the pregnancy he most likely be an emotionally straightforward and supportive father during birth. The point of most of the preparation was so that the opening night goes very smoothly and without a hitch. He will find just the right balance of personal assertiveness and cue-taking from the mother.

Omega Stage

The Cast Party: All of the cast and crew will be invited to a housewarming party where they can celebrate the successful performance. This father will make sure that everyone, especially the mother, gets the proper recuperation needed. The binder may be put in a place of special importance with some mementos from the birth with it.

Evil Twins

The Control Freak: No one moves or speaks without his direct or indirect approval.

The Prima Donna: I have seen a few stage managers who associate with overly dramatic actors, of which both the actor and the stage manager try to make it all about them. Flamboyant behavior, attention seeking actions, and the occasional childish antics will only distract the mother from laboring.

The Daniel Boone

Daniel Boone was a famous early American frontiersman who lived from 1734 to 1820. The best way I can define frontiersman is by comparing it to the modern concept of a survivalist, but in a landscape that had both Native Americans and Europeans who could decide at any time to either be his ally or kill him. Not only was he an explorer and used to living on his own in an unmapped part of Virginia (by Europeans anyway), but he and his wife eventually had ten children while living in North Carolina.

I am not comparing birth to hunting and skinning animals. However, there are many different types of fluids in different levels of abundance at a normal birth. It is also a common conception that many men pass out or faint at the sight of blood. The Daniel Boone role is exactly the opposite. Nothing will faze this guy and he will do whatever it takes to ensure the mother's mental well-being and physical health.

This father doesn't have the medical knowledge of an EMT per se, but he will not be swayed by any deviation in the birth plan. If the cell phone goes out at the hospital, he'll pick an office lock to use the building phone to call the in-laws. If at home or another locale, he will boil water with a lighter, use his shirt as a cloth, and pay no mind to the blood and other assorted birth fluids.

Symbol: The Multi-Tool. You never know when you are going to need it.

Alpha Stage

Many women are put off by this father early in the pregnancy, as it may seem he is uninterested in the impending birth. In truth, he is aware of the general gist of what will happen and is steeling himself for any and all eventualities - to play it by ear so to speak. It is very difficult, early in the pregnancy, to distinguish this father from a seemingly lazy one. This father may nest during the pregnancy, a sign that he is mentally preparing for the upcoming labor. He will be very hands on, for example: he will assemble the birthing tub or birth hammock, no problem, or build anything else related.

Labor (Stages 1-3)

This father won't be content to sit there and hold his wife's hand during the pushing stage. He will most likely know how, and want to, check the dilation of the cervix, what station the baby is at, and be involved in all the other stages of labor. It may be hard for the mother to distinguish her husband from the attending OB or midwife (if there is one, as this is another role that is more suited to home and 3rd party locale births). During the labor he will very excited about what is going on, will let the mother know how well she is doing, and how much he enjoys this part of labor. When the baby is born, he will be very reassuring and will finally let his excitement loose when he hands the newborn to his wife.

Omega Stage

After the birth, this role will morph into the storyteller. He will tell relative after relative, and friend after friend, about all the hairy and exciting details of every part of the birth - while holding his infant for added visual aid. There will be plenty of time for the mother to rest while he is reliving his great adventure to his audience, and at times, she may have to insist on getting the infant back so she can spend time nursing and bonding herself. The only issue for the mother and this role may be getting him to do some chores around the house in between stories.

Evil Twins

The Emergency Room Doctor: I must be careful here again to say that this type of personality is not bad in and of itself, but if a father were to treat his laboring wife as if she had just walked in the door and did not know anything about her personally, it would be very upsetting to the mother. This father would need to remember he is there for his wife first, the adventure second.

The Butcher: This father might actually get so caught up in the physicality of birth, the digging right in so to speak, that he may forget to attend to his wife mentally and emotionally. Distraction can come in many forms, and could affect this role more easily than the rest.

The Firmin Richard

In 1909, Gaston Leroux published a book called *Le Fantôme de l'Opéra*, known in the English speaking world as the *Phantom of the Opera*. The plot revolves around a physically deformed architect, Erik, who helped design the Paris Opera House. Erik helps a young woman named Christine, to become a talented opera singer. An ensuing drama of romance follows where he at first kidnaps and tries to force Christine to marry him, but then lets her marry her childhood sweetheart.

Among the characters of this novel are the two producers of the Paris Opera House, Armand Moncharmin and Firmin Richard. It was their job to make sure that the musical directors, the actors, and the all the crewmembers of the Opera House had the provisions and equipment necessary to put on successful operas. This role is a combination of the Euripides and the Sir Charles Berkeley, but is different from the latter in terms that the mother wants this father there as much as possible for the labor and delivery.

This father really wants to be a part of the action when it happens, even if he lacks the proper experience. He makes sure that the mother is aware they he has the money issues taken care of, and also of his desire and extreme interest in the birth. Despite all that, he can still only just sit back and watch after all the preparations are made. It is not his fault; it may be the only way he can feel comfortable at the birth. This can be one of the least present fathers, but the concern is still there. This is the best role for the father whose main concern is finances and paying for/providing all the best services out there.

It is common knowledge that some people in the world are much better off than others. I will not get into the how or why, but just deal with the fact that some fathers out there have the desire and resources to express their devotion to their pregnant and laboring wives through financial and material means. There is no judgment here, any way that a father can help his wife feel more supported in labor is up to him alone.

Symbol: The Daily Appointment Planner. This father may always keep his checkbook or plastic cards ready, but it is more important to him to know that anyone helping his wife is not failing in their promptness and duties.

Alpha Stage

This father may not be into the book reading and classes as much, but he will want to talk to his wife about every little detail of what she may experience or need for the entire pregnancy and delivery. Stress relief for both him and the mother will most likely be handled very well. The option of doulas and massage therapists will not be an issue.

Labor (Stages 1-3)

This father will probably feel most comfortable as the closest bystander possible. The old cliché of the hand-holding bewildered husband is most likely best suited for this role. It is entirely possible that this father will spend the pregnancy as the opera producer, and then for the labor step into a nursing or active coaching role. Even though there may be doulas, masseuses, and other assistants, it does not have to keep this father from taking a very active role himself once the producing is done. However, the mother should not be upset if he bounces between the two extremes.

Omega Stage

Take out and dine-in food, laundry service, postpartum doulas, babysitters - this may be the time where this father may spend the most money. There is a certain satisfaction to being able to procure total comfort and sanctity for the minimum two weeks of recuperation and rest for the mother.

Evil Twin

The Silent Partner: This father will simply throw some money at the situation and then go back about his own business. Leaving the mother to handle the finances, pregnancy, labor, and two weeks recovery by herself is one of the worst ways a father could support his wife.

The Cicero

Cicero was a skilled Roman politician and lawyer. He also wrote on a wide variety of subjects. His topics included, but were not limited to, friendship, rhetoric, divination, law, the nature of gods and politics. The man had a way with words, to say the least. He also exercised considerable political clout during a time of great upheaval in Rome, which was the time of Julius Caesar. He had a skill for knowing exactly what was going on, and had the cunning and cleverness to make sure that he got his way; or at the very least, to have his voice heard.

This role would best suit the personalities that are a combination of attentive observers, assertive protectors, and strong verbal types. He is extremely present and involved. This is the role that is probably the easiest for fathers out there to relate to. However, a certain charm is needed to pull this role off.

Like the opera producer Firmin Richard, it may be hard at times to distinguish this father from the basic lazy one. However, it is not the wife's responsibility to look for the distinctions. It is up to the father in all of these roles to demonstrate his desire to be a willing participant in the pregnancy and labor. For the Cicero role, his knowledge of the birth coupled with his charm may put the mother at ease.

Symbol: The Glass. This father will always have something close and handy to drink. It does not have to be alcohol either. His beverage may help by either giving off calm vibes, or to coolly sip while he is thinking about his next move.

Alpha Stage

This is the type of father who actually paid attention to all the small things mentioned to him throughout his life about pregnancy and birth. Books and classes may seem like review to him. He may not bring up too many questions with his wife, but will not hesitate to talk thoroughly about anything that she asks him.

Labor (Stages 1-3)

This father is mostly hands-off until something happens that deviates from the birth plan or is against the wishes of the mother, whether she is incapacitated or not. If he is not a lawyer, he will have one ready by a phone somewhere, or on retainer. The lawyer part is probably only needed if the birth is in a hospital, as it is no lie that many hospitals view consent as a quaint illusion. All external and preventative measures or contingencies – will be locked down. There will be no distractions or anxiety at this birth. The Cicero is not so much about just following orders, but calm anticipation, and adamant follow through. Safety and security are the foremost concerns of this father, even though he may not show it during labor.

Omega Stage

Now that there is a new arrival in this father's house, monitoring is task number one. The calm anticipation mentioned earlier will come in very handy here, as he will be the first to notice when the mother needs anything, be it rest or a distracting activity. The infant will not go a second in need without this father quietly arriving at the scene and meeting every need without complaint. He won't need much help from friends and family, as they may present loose ends or have a few negative effects on the two people (or more if this isn't the first child) he cares about most in the world.

Evil Twins

The Inquisitor: This is the dad who heard or read about way too many birth horror stories. He will serve as the bodyguard for the mother and intercept any person other than the midwife who wishes to approach the laboring mother. He will ask the hospital staff many questions with a suspicious tone and still not trust them in the end. This husband presents a serious challenge to the wife, as she will have to spend a large amount of time convincing him to trust, for the most part, the people and professionals that she trusts.

The Mute Brute: There is such a thing as too strong or too silent.

The Orpheus

In Greek myth, Orpheus was a legendary poet and musician. One of his most famous stories tells of how his wife, Eurydice, died after being bit by a viper. Orpheus was so distraught that he traveled to the underworld to convince Hades and Persephone to let him bring Eurydice back to the world of the living. He played a song so sad that even the King and Queen of the underworld were moved to tears and granted his wish. This story shows elements of strong outward love and a deep connection with a significant other.

The inspiration of this role, however, is based on a personality type that I like to call the soul gazer. This is the extremely emotionally supportive husband who is comfortable holding his wife's hands and staring into her eyes for over six hours, and can keep her soul from descending into the deep dark depths of despair. He usually could care less about most of what is going on more than eight inches from his wife's head. He may border on the New Age or hippie type, but most times not.

Fortunately for husbands like this, the wife loves him for these very traits outside of, and before the birth - so this attitude is welcome during labor. He will spend most of the alpha stage and labor being very communicative with the wife about her feelings and expectations. He is a hopeless romantic, but more a talker and holder, as opposed to the sweep you off your feet Jean Baptiste Lully. This father is a psychologist, therapist, and cheerleader all wrapped up into one personality type.

Symbol: The Breath Mints, or breath freshening gum. He will spend most of the labor either holding his wife or being face to face with her guiding her through the contractions. These items will be of utmost importance, and he will have plenty.

Alpha Stage

This father borders very closely to a yes man, but luckily for the wife, he will stand up for her in the delivery room, no matter the cost or opposition. Having said that, he will most likely just quietly attend all the birth classes with a pleasant smile on his face, and then listen intently to his wife's concerns and interests on the drives home. He will enjoy going out of his way to make nice and healthy meals for the mother's dietary changes during pregnancy. He will be quietly anxious and ready when the first stage of labor begins, and may be so wrapped in his wife's emotions that he may notice it before her.

Labor (Stages 1-3)

This father will be adept at using empowering mental imagery and visualizations, for example, describing a waterfall during a contraction. He is very good at helping with all the labor movements and positions, culminating in his expertise with the birth dance, which can be an umbrella term for all the different movements a mother goes through during the end of the first and also the second stage of labor. This is the role that could come as close as possible to actual empathy with the mother during labor. True empathy may never occur since he is not a woman. However, sensing and feeling her emotions, along with physically being able to feel the body movement due to his closeness with her, will give him a unique perspective on the birthing process.

Omega Stage

There will be no ceremonies or rituals for this father. No calls to the family or stories to the friends. He will spend most of the two weeks of recovery time either snuggling with the baby, snuggling with the wife while she rests, or doing everything that needs to be done around the house - all with a genuine and gentle smile on his face.

Evil Twins

The Weeper: This is the father who cries more than the mother. Tears may flow when the wind changes direction. However, this is probably the rarest of all the evil twins.

The Yes-Robot: Society has a certain tolerance for yes men. When it's just mindless and soulless, there is a line being crossed somehow.

The Walt Whitman

Walt Whitman was well known as a great American writer. What is not well known is that before he was a writer, he was a nurse during the American Civil War. The existence of a nurse-poet serves as the inspiration for this role, which I originally named the triage saint. Some fathers out there may already be EMTs, doctors, nurses, or practice in some other medically related field. When it comes times for the pregnancy and labor, there will be not much of anything new to learn about the biological process of birth.

The special quality that is useful for birth however, is that this role also takes into account the personal touch of his wife's unique personality. This father may have the upper hand over most non-medically trained fathers, but that does not excuse him from any of the supportive and emotional aspects of the birth. That is why the poet part of the role is necessary. It is also possible for a father to choose and develop this role with no prior medical knowledge before the pregnancy.

Symbol: The Uniform. Hospital scrubs, or a chosen set of clothes worn especially for labor. Even if the birth is not in a hospital, a uniform will represent his readiness to help the laboring mother in any way. If the birth is at a hospital, he may be wearing scrubs so he can blend in and move among the staff like a secret agent.

Alpha Stage

This father may get a layman's medical degree in the first two trimesters and is ready for any and all possible birth outcomes. After his first pregnancy, he could be hired as an EMT. Like the title implies, he can grasp, anticipate, and handle almost any medical situation within a general uncomplicated birth.

This father will take notes and discuss things with the physician or midwife, almost like an apprentice. He will read all the class textbooks, the birth books, as well as general medical books. He may delight in discussing all the medical choices with the mother and getting a good feel for how she wants things to go.

Labor (Stages 1-3)

It may be hard to separate this father from all the other medical staff, but a good husband will take any extra time needed to tender to his wife's mental and emotional needs first, before he goes back to medically assisting the labor. He may be very methodical, yet he may add that perfect and highly enjoyable personal touch that many women, who choose to labor in a hospital, desire.

This father may even help administer the Apgar tests and help with the 3rd stage of labor, which means helping with the delivery of the placenta. He will always ensure that the mother has all her needs met first.

Omega Stage

During the recovery phase, this father's primary efforts will be twofold: first, he will ensure that the baby's vitals, weight, skin color, etc., are textbook in their diagnosis. Second, he will most likely insist that the mother stay on bed rest within their home while he makes sure she and the baby are regaining the rest and fluids that they need. The only downside is that he may fall behind a tad in the day to day logistics. Health is first and foremost.

Evil Twin

The Exam Crammer: It is possible, early in the pregnancy, for a father to choose this role and not follow through with the massive amount of study and learning that it requires to be very familiar with the mountain of details that can sometimes accompany any type of birth. He may come around at the last minute and cram like it's a college 101 exam. When it comes times for labor he may be the total kind of useless, both physically and mentally.

The Tristan

While many know of the more famous knights of the King Arthur myths such as Lancelot and Percival, Tristan was one of the more popular ones during medieval times. His main story was a love romance with an Irish maiden named Iseult. Tristan was sent to retrieve her for King Mark of Cornwall. On the way back they both ingested a potion that caused them to fall in love with each other. The knight's resolve and sense of honor are tested many times in the ensuing story.

The reason I chose this Arthurian knight is that he best represents the man trying to grasp all that is going on around him, constantly thinking, but who somehow manages to get his head around it at the end and save day. His morals and courage are strong, but he finds himself in a situation that tests his resolve in a romantic way. I believe that this heroic attitude can be applied to a role during pregnancy and birth.

This is the most delicate role I've developed, as it is the easiest to mistake for the uncaring and distant father. If there was ever a father who spent the pregnancy only half-thinking and being unsure about what was going to happen at birth, only to then rise up to the occasion and become a hero to his laboring wife, this would be that role.

To paraphrase the main character in the movie *Knocked Up*, there can be some basic and instinctive approaches to birth. Prior to the printing press, there weren't really a lot of material for fathers to read. Some of us may take for granted the massive amount of books today about pregnancy and birth, even if they are mostly written by and for women. On the flip side, however, this is only a starting point; a father cannot go through the entire pregnancy and birth just winging it.

Despite the mother making this father watch multiple real birth videos, read many books, look at diagrams and anatomy models – this person still may not be able to wrap their head around the whole birth process until much later in the pregnancy, perhaps towards the very end of the Alpha Stage.

Symbol: The Stress Ball. This father may be often seen twirling or fidgeting with some object either due to intense thought, confusion, or anxiety.

Alpha Stage

It is not that this father won't read any books, or not go to classes during the pregnancy; it's just that when the mother wishes to talk to him about it, he probably won't have much to say. This father is not stupid or lazy, he just has a slow information absorption rate. For some people, the theory becomes clear when the situation demands it. It is as simple as that. It may be frustrating for the mother during the nine months prior to the big day, but the person who truly fits into this role will find ways to reassure his wife that he is taking the materials and the discussions about the upcoming birth seriously.

Labor (Stages 1-3)

These fathers may always look bewildered. Some of these types can hit a bull's-eye with a sniper rifle in high wind - but may be jittery at the birth. If he is self-aware, he will occasionally catch himself acting nervous, and will step outside to get some air and calm down. On the flip side, after the baby is born, he may be the most ecstatic and cathartic of all the new fathers. Luckily, for most couples, they were well aware of this personality trait long before pregnancy and have no problem ignoring it.

It is my belief that the longer the father finds himself surrounded by the processes of labor and birth, the more he will become comfortable and rise to the occasion. At the beginning of the first stage of labor, he may look nervous or quiet, but it probably won't take long for him to find his own confidence and exude that same willpower to his laboring wife. By the time this minor transformation happens, he will be borderline overly enthusiastic. He may be totally exhilarated by the entire process.

Omega Stage

This is the only role where the qualities and attributes that the father exhibits during the Alpha and Labor stages can differ completely from the Omega Stage. It is hard to predict how this father will act during this period. It is a safe bet that he won't look bewildered or feel nervous. My best guess is that this father may turn into a psychology student and spend the time that the mother is resting totally studying the infant in all its infinite moods, needs, and desires.

Evil Twin

The Caffeine Blur: This father may make the mistake of believing that the more caffeine he has, the better he will understand what is going with his wife and her labor.

The Nicholas Culpeper

Nicholas Culpeper lived in England from 1616 to 1654, and wrote books on such subjects as medicine, herbalism, botany, astrology, etc. The profession that many in the west today would call a doctor had a much different connotation in the 1600s. This man was a physician but used a large variety of methods, both mainstream and alternative relative to the time period, to heal the sick. It is worth noting, with a sense of irony, that he died at a young age due to tuberculosis.

This father can be a master of, or simply dabble in, herbalism, homeopathy, naturopathy, yoga, meditation, etc. – all of the above or any combination. It is very rare to catch this father and the mother in a hospital. This father is completely on board with his wife's choice of a home or third-party locale birth. He will be very knowledgeable on many different types of birth techniques. His holistic leanings can either be supplemental or in place of the allopathic methods, if they find themselves in a hospital. This role is not anti-hospital, but does prefer and enjoy additional and supplemental ideas and procedures.

Symbol: The Backpack. This father will have some sort of comfortable carrying case that may have simple healing remedies or different vitamins for varying occasions. A bottle of water and tea may also be in there, but not necessarily.

Alpha Stage

Diet is crucial for this father, and for good reason. Most of the birth books I read, even by other fathers, stressed the importance of good diet during the pregnancy. Most likely they already have a well-established healthy diet, and it will not be difficult to further it tweak it for additional calories, vitamins, proteins, minerals, etc. It not that the other roles ignore the importance of diet, it is just that this is the father that will excel above most of the others at it.

Stress management issues will most likely be expressed through alternative concepts such as yoga, art therapy, and herbalism, for example, drinking relaxing teas. Communication can be easily maintained through enjoyable exercises such as walking, when there is ample opportunity to talk about things pregnancy and life related.

Labor (Stages 1-3)

This birth partner can be well versed in the multitude of alternative and non-traditional pain relief methods. Sheila Kitzinger, lists many of these methods: hypnosis, acupuncture, transcutaneous electronic nerve stimulation (TENS), reflexology, aromatherapy, and homeopathic remedies.

Different breathing methods will also be a favorite topic for this father, and he may go to great lengths to help the pregnant mother pick out and practice the best ones for her. He may have different flavored ice chips and herb scented wet washcloths for the labor. In *Polly's Birth Book*, I found some interesting sections on pressure points that can help the mother during labor, as well as references to multiple forms of hydrotherapy.

This father does not have to be an expert on any of these or even do them himself. He can provide an expert in any of these fields to be present at the birth. For my wife's fourth birth, my first, I made sure to have a professional massage therapist there for the back pain, and she did have her work cut out for her.

Omega Stage

The healing and recuperating stage will be just as important to this father as the birth itself. Diet and rest will be the primary focus, for everyone, possibly even himself, just as it was during the alpha and labor stages. Since most of the lifestyle choices were most likely already in action before the birth, only minor adjustments, such as different types of teas and very low impact exercises, will be tweaked. The mother will have no shortage of nourishment and rest for at least two weeks.

Evil Twins

The Super Hippie: This father may believe and try anything out there that slightly resembles a health product. Any new fringe and wild medical theories, which borders on snake oil, will excite him greatly. This attitude will not help the mother as chances are he will simply only be interested in the pregnancy and birth as a perfect time to try all these neat and cool things out, with little regard to the mother's actual well-being.

The Medical Conspiracy Theorist: This is the father that is pretty much anti-hospital and will not take seriously anything that sounds allopathic. He will probably hold anyone in that profession with total disdain. Again, this is not helpful to the mother in that she may want to keep all available options open to her just in case there is a true medical emergency, as most of us would.

The Hannibal

Hannibal was what we would loosely call a General, and lived from 247 to 182 BC. He was in charge of the army of Carthage, and is most famous for waging several successful battles against the Roman Republic. Even though he was a brilliant military strategist, Rome would emerge the victor of the Punic Wars. He was so talented that he even had the respect of many Romans.

This role takes its inspiration from types of men who are very powerful, yet still removed, most of the time anyway, from the real action. This is the role for fathers who decide they can't, or don't want to be, at the labor for any reason. He still wants to be as involved as he can, even if he is not there by her side. As opposed to the Sir Charles Berkeley, the decision to not be there is his, even though he may change his mind partway throughout the labor. This role does not apply to those who wish to be out golfing, at the bar, at a sporting event, or at work.

Unfortunately, this father makes the best target for hospitals with statistical agendas, or OB's with scheduling agendas. That is why I chose Hannibal as the inspiration for this role, so that no fathers will be bullied by anyone at the birth, be it medical, family, or otherwise, just because he is not in the room with the mother herself.

Symbol: The Clipboard, with vitals and any possible pertinent medical information, as well as choices and preferences if the mother is declared incapacitated. The birth plan would most likely be on the clipboard as well.

Alpha Stage

This father will put a lot of effort into the birth plan. It will be his main source of effort during the alpha stage. It goes without saying that the birth plan may become very detailed and well thought out. He will go into the birth removed, yet highly informed in his own way. He may become familiar with local relevant laws concerning consent and what is considered a medical emergency. He will see and prepare for all possible choices, outcomes, and situations – like a military strategist with a chessboard.

Labor (Stages 1-3)

This father will want a Situation Room, for him alone. A hallway or corner of a lobby will not suffice. This space will be similar to the R.W. Emerson's sacred space. He may go as far as to view the mother and infant as soldiers in battle. Any General was a soldier once himself, and will be prepared to revert to a soldier at any time, if he changes his mind and decides to attend the labor.

Omega Stage

This father will go to great lengths to ensure that the mother and her child did not suffer any negative effects or results from the place and attendees of the birth. If so, there will be hell to pay, and he will also make sure that the mother and baby get the care they need. If everything goes to plan and both the mother and child are fine, he will be extremely thankful. He will not complain and do all the day to day stuff very stoically and gratefully as the mother and child spend as much time as they need to recover and recuperate.

Evil Twins

The Golfer: named in honor of the dad from the movie *She's Having a Baby*, the father who does not want to be near or a part of the birth, and will be engaging in another activity until the birth is over. Maybe it's too much of a woman thing, or he is too good for it.

The Agathon

The *Symposium* was a dialogue written by Plato, in which he ponders the nature of love and philosophy. The focus for this role is not the discussion of the nature of love per se, but the *Symposium* itself. Academics describe the dialogue in many ways, but one certainty is that it was a sophisticated party where serious matters were discussed and social ceremonies were celebrated. The host of the drinking party was Agathon. In essence, since the symposium took place at his house and he was the master of ceremonies. He was the host, the one responsible for the well-being of his attendees.

In the spirit of Agathon, this father may turn the birth into a ritual, spectator sport, festival, and televised event – all at the same time. He channels most of his energy into making the birth a boisterous and joyous event. He will make sure that all the medical and logistical details are well taken care of early, so that the mother can relax and birth her own way. He may want to spend the birth supporting his wife like John Madden in a delivery room, with all his family and friends in another room enjoying appetizers and waiting for the presentation of the newborn. If he is clever, he will ask the visitors to help clean the house before they all leave.

In the book *A Man's Place: Masculinity and the Middle-Class Home in Victorian England*, we find an interesting excerpt: "Childbirth came to be seen as the fulfillment of a woman's femininity rather than a disruption to her performance of the duties of wife. This was one reason why the prestige of motherhood was on the increase, and it meant that the mother as bearer of the child became the central figure, rather than the father as bearer of the family name. Instead of being the master of ceremonies and focus of public attention, the father was on the way to becoming the nervous bystander of recent times."

I believe that this attitude can be refitted to modern times. This father is about marking the occasion, making arrangements, getting proper help, involving people, and being involved. Such examples can be calls to the friends and family, organizing the post-labor baby meets, making comfortable travel arrangements to and from the birth location, and lining up babysitters for the Omega

Stage. These fathers are the social butterflies of birth, but still walk that line of taking it very seriously.

It isn't about having parties, it's about having fun and being involved by marking the occasions and using those situations as opportunities to bond with the mother and baby, in any way that feels comfortable to him. This role differs from the R.W. Emerson in that the rituals are private. For this role, they are more akin to public ceremony. The difference could be viewed as spiritual vs. secular outlooks.

Symbol: This father's symbol is the same as the Firmin Richard, The Daily Planner. In this scenario, it is used more for keeping track of family and friends, and less importance is on the hired services.

Alpha Stage

After the positive pregnancy test, this father will go to great lengths to make the mother feel like the center of attention for the remainder of the pregnancy and the birth. When they receive the good news on having a child he will probably take her out to a special and sentimental dinner or other romantic occasion, one that will not easily be forgotten.

He may buy cigars, champagne, and many other things to mark the occasion. He should hold his wife up on a pedestal as the main social attraction of the party. In essence, he may enjoy putting together and hosting the announcement gathering, but he will make it clear that it is about the expectant mother and the fun times she is going to have for the next nine or ten months.

When the mother first starts showing symptoms he may pause, show some inner reflection, show signs of relief, and start developing routines or idiosyncrasies that will help the mother deal with the effects of pregnancy. He may look forward to the impending scheduling and including of friends and family to help out during the next nine months.

This father will also take the first prenatal appointment very seriously. He will be eager to know what type of birth the mother will be choosing, which is almost like choosing a venue. If the birth is going to occur in a hospital his questions to the doctor or midwife will be in the interest of what will be going on all around the wife during labor, and his freedom to move around and interact. He might be feeling the medical staff out for his ability to flit about the delivery area like a socialite at a grand ballroom.

If a home or third party locale is chosen, then all gloves are off and he can really out-do himself in the planning and preparations for the next eight months. This father will definitely remember the date and rhythm of the heartbeat if they have the option to listen. It is unlikely that physical symptoms of couvade will start to develop, but the mental symptoms may be more likely to appear.

The financial logistics of pregnancy probably won't be the utmost concern in this role. The stress release leading up to the pregnancy for this role does not have to mean going out to a social outing or having friends over. It is not that everything needs to be marked with a social occasion, but a few huge ones might help him better navigate the journey. The same goes for communication. This father will be able to talk to the mother during pregnancy and labor in a one-on-one setting. Most of the energies of this father will be during the Alpha and Omega Stages.

This father may even want to assemble a group of women attendants for the event, such as family and friends, resembling how mothers labored in the centuries before hospital births.

Labor (Stages 1-3)

During the labor, this father will most likely take the basic role of coach. However, he will be making mental notes of all the important milestones during the delivery. That way, he can celebrate them later, during the Omega Stage.

Omega Stage

Luckily for the mother, this father will know when it's proper to celebrate the new addition to the family with, and without her. He will probably give great detail to planning any social event *around* her recuperation schedule. It goes without saying that many favors will be called to help out with the day to day logistics around the house so that he may tend to the mother and baby's sleep and rest schedule.

Evil Twins

The Frat Boy: The father who gets too caught up in the socializing and revelry, talking to the medical staff or laymen attendants, and loses track of his wife's condition or progression.

The Boozer: Sadly some fathers may take any occasion as an excuse to have a drink, in the guise of a celebratory gesture.

Chapter Ten
Odds and Ends

When we reviewed the information from the books, we also came across little tidbits of knowledge that might be useful in our quest to develop roles for fathers during birth. Even though the scope for this book was specific, everyone loves fun facts to know and tell. These examples include topics that are relevant, but so far do not fit anywhere else in the development of the roles of fathers during birth. Here is supplemental information listed for the continued development and adaptation of the roles that were presented earlier.

These subjects, facts, and ideas are for offering perspective, and may actually be helpful outside of the roles offered. This chapter is also about thinking outside the box and not viewing birth as some far off and alien experience. Please forgive the format, as it may be short and jumpy. Some of the topics may also be too controversial to be addressed in the role development. This is the only other chapter with medical definitions and terminology, but only so that you are not talked down to or viewed as ignorant by hospital staff, birth center attendants, midwives, and doulas during the birth.

What follows are mostly my opinions and observations on unique birth related topics. Parents are meant to follow my lead in finding out how they feel about these topics, not to take my word as absolute truth.

Drugs and Chemicals

Most would be surprised at just how many chemicals are involved in childbirth. I'm not just talking about the drugs used at hospitals either. Here are some examples and how they relate to labor and delivery. Some are naturally occurring while others are manufactured.

168

- Oxytocin: A hormone secreted by the pituitary gland that stimulates uterine contractions during labor and stimulates milk glands in the breasts to produce milk.[60] It is also found in male semen, which seems to be Mother Nature's way of saying that sex may help bring on labor. Pitocin is a synthetic form of this same hormone, but has a different action when injected. Maybe hospitals frown upon sex in the delivery rooms...
- Dextrose: A solution of glucose used to supplement the level of blood sugar, usually introduced by intravenous drip during a long hospital birth.[61]
- Prostaglandins: another hormone found in semen that can help induce labor. The synthetic form is Cervadil or Misoprostol, which is also known as Cytotec.
- Progesterone: A hormone produced by the placenta. Among many things, it is useful for the health of the uterus. Its synthetic form is progestogen.
- Prolactin: A hormone that stimulates milk production for breast-feeding.[62]
- Catecholamines: Stress hormones produced by the mother and baby during labor that play an important part in preparing the baby for birth.[63]

Couvade

This term has been causing quite a stir among academics studying fathers and birth. Even its true definition is being debated. The best summary I found was by Richard K. Reed:

"So how do we understand couvade? Is it a neurotic attempt to do with sublimated drives, as is suggested by the medical literature, or is it a ritual preparation of the father for his new child? American Medical research has limited its exploration of couvade to its individual expression and its psychological roots. Thus limited, it explains fathers' reactions

---

[60] Kitzinger, *The Complete Book of Pregnancy and Childbirth,* 432
[61] Kitzinger, *The Complete Book of Pregnancy and Childbirth,* 430
[62] Kitzinger, *The Complete Book of Pregnancy and Childbirth,* 433
[63] Kitzinger, *The Complete Book of Pregnancy and Childbirth,* 429

as signs of a flawed constitution. If we understand these activities as a culturally patterned social process, however, then we uncover a fundamentally different level of meanings. Increasingly, midwives - who reject many of the medical approaches to women's pregnancy - are becoming aware that fathers share pregnancy and express it in both body and action (Gaskin 2003; Davis-Floyd and Saint John 1998). Thus, we can see couvade as a constructive and proactive preparation for the coming of a new child."[64]

Some of the most common examples of this condition are weight gain, morning sickness, and food cravings. A few fathers have even reported feeling sympathy pains. My opinion is that fathers should not be embarrassed or ashamed if they feel any signs of empathy or sympathy with the mother during pregnancy, biological, emotional, or otherwise.

Terms and Definitions (non-technological or biological)

- Tocophobia: the fear of pregnancy, and may also be called "maieusiophobia".
- Dystocia: A diagnostic term for prolonged or difficult labor.
- Shoulder dystocia: A state in which the baby's shoulders get stuck during delivery.[65]
- Preeclampsia (Pre-E , Preeclamptic toxemia, or PET): An illness in which a woman has high blood pressure, edema, protein in the urine, and often sudden excessive weight gain.
- Braxton-Hicks Contractions/prodromal labor/false labor: (rehearsal) contractions of the uterus that occur throughout the pregnancy, but which may not be noticed until toward the end.[66]
- Cephalopelvic Disproportion (CPD): when the head is too big for the pelvis. The percentage of this truly occurring is a point of contention among many studies.
- D and C: The surgical dilation (opening) of the cervix and the curettage (removal of the contents) of the uterus.[67]

---

[64] Reed, *Birthing Fathers: The Transformation of Men in American Rites of Birth*, 74

[65] Kitzinger, *The Complete Book of Pregnancy and Childbirth*, 430

[66] Kitzinger, *The Complete Book of Pregnancy and Childbirth*, 429

- External cephalic version (ECV or version): is a procedure used to attempt to turn a fetus from a breech position or side-lying (transverse) position into a head-down (vertex) position before labor begins.[68]
- Intrauterine growth restriction (IUGR): "refers to the poor growth of a baby while in the mother's womb during pregnancy. Specifically, it means the developing baby weighs less than 90% of other babies at the same gestational age."[69]
- Low Amniotic Fluid: refers to the amount of amniotic fluid that the baby has inside the uterus. This can be a sign of kidney problems, however it is truly difficult to know what is too low because each pregnancy is different.

Biology

While reading all the different pregnancy books, I came to the conclusion that there are only so many different ways an author can describe the same medical information. Don't get me wrong, each pregnancy and birth is extremely unique, and there is tons of medical trivia that physicians need to memorize. Having said that, most pregnancy birth books walk their readers through the same medical path. In order to challenge myself, I recorded the interesting tidbits that I would find in one book and not another. A lot of this information slips through the publishing cracks, which is disappointing, as some of them may be very important to many parents.

- Apgar Scale: A general test of the baby's well-being given immediately after the birth to ascertain the heart rate and tone, respiration, blood circulation, and nerve responses.[70]

---

[67] Kitzinger, *The Complete Book of Pregnancy and Childbirth,* 430

[68] "External Cephalic Version (Version) for Breech Position," WedMD, last modified July 25, 2011, http://www.webmd.com/baby/external-cephalic-version-version-for-breech-position

[69] "Intrauterine growth restriction," PubMed Health, last modified November 8, 2012, http://www.ncbi.nlm.nih.gov/pubmedhealth/PMH0002469/

[70] Kitzinger, *The Complete Book of Pregnancy and Childbirth,* 429

- Delayed umbilical cord clamping and cutting: Up to a 1/3rd of all of the baby's blood can be in the placenta after the birth; the length of time that it takes to go back to the baby varies.
- Umbilical Cords: As long as the material is sterile, parents can use anything they want to cut the umbilical cord after it has been clamped. I have heard of fathers using hunting knives to family heirloom knives. Many mothers like to make their own ties for the cord.
- Boys average 100 more minutes for labor.
- Women's brains shrink 5% and can suffer decent short term memory loss during pregnancy.
- The vagina swells and changes color during pregnancy and birth; it can turn darker pink to a light purple.
- About 90% to 95% of births do not happen on the exact due date, 3 of 10 before, 7 of 10 after, but all usually within 10 days.
- There are pressure points to relieve pain during labor. There are some pregnancy books and guides that illustrate which pressure points on the body can help with certain kinds of labor pains.
- A Lotus Birth is when the umbilical cord is not cut after the child is born. The placenta is carried around in a special basket until the cord falls off itself.
- A lot of laboring women find it useful to have frequent bathroom breaks during labor.
- There's an actual book about all the uses of the placenta alone, including various ways of ingesting it. The book is called *Placenta: The Gift of Life*, by Cornelia Enning.
- There is such a thing as a birth orgasm.
- Meconium: The first contents of the bowel, present in the fetus before birth and passed during the first few days after birth. The presence of meconium in the amniotic fluid before delivery is usually taken as a sign of fetal distress.[71]

---

[71] Kitzinger, *The Complete Book of Pregnancy and Childbirth*, 432

Circumcisions

During my research, I read articles that both praise and condemn circumcisions. Most articles focus on the medical and cultural aspects. All agree that ultimately it is up to the parents to make that choice for the newly born son. My son is not circumcised. My wife believed that it was not her choice, that it was indeed his choice, to make a decision that would alter his body significantly. My reason for not having it done was different than most. I believe my argument may shed some new light on the debate.

Nipples. While in the womb, both male and female fetuses develop six nipples. For the large majority of the fetuses, four of these nipples 'go away'. We know this due to gestational studies and also that not all of those extra nipples go away all the time. There is a decent percentage of the human population born with an extra nipple. The medical term relating to this is atavism.

Nipples are related to human sexuality and reproduction. The foreskin is also related to human sexuality and reproduction. My argument is that Mother Nature removed the parts relating to sexuality and reproduction that she did not deem necessary. If the foreskin was not removed during gestation, as the extra four nipples usually are, then Mother Nature deems the foreskin necessary, like the remaining two nipples. I decided to put my trust in that Mother Nature left the foreskin on my son for a reason, even if I don't know what that reason is. Mother Nature must know something; she got rid of those other four nipples, right? If my nipple vs. foreskin argument doesn't convince you, just search the internet for vestigial tail.

Myths and Perceptions

There are many urban legends that accompany stories about labor and delivery. Some of them are severe and can make a mother very anxious, if taken seriously. Others are silly and only serve to make some fathers even more nervous during labor. Since one of the goals in this book is to make the father familiar and comfortable enough with birth to develop his own unique role, it goes without question that I should spend a little bit of time dispelling some of the more popular myths and negative perceptions.

Myth: Birth is **always** painful. *Truth*: Overwhelming birth pain can be caused by many non-natural factors. Some examples are being forced to labor in an incorrect position, given too much Pitocin or any at all.

Myth: Pregnancy and birth are dangerous conditions. Author Richard K. Reed explained how hospitals diagnose pregnant woman as an aberrant condition that needs to be cured. *Truth*: Pregnancy and birth are very normal and natural events that have very low percentages of complications.

Myth: Eating or drinking before or during labor can have harmful effects on the mother and infant. *Truth*: Doctors do not want women in labor to eat food in case they end up needing to be knocked out for a cesarean section. This is a leftover behavior from the mid-century when doctors were worried they would vomit and aspirate their food. Studies have shown that this is extremely rare, and that the acid from an empty stomach is worse on the lungs than food. Another drawback to not eating during the entire labor, is that it can dehydrate and tire the mother before the baby is born.

Myth: Vaginal births after cesarean (VBACs) are dangerous. *Truth*: Studies are showing that they are safe, and there can be more complications from repeated C-sections than VBACs.

Myth: Jaundice indicates a problem with the newborn. *Truth*: It is actually quite common and natural in newborns and is not a reason to stop breastfeeding or to add anything to the newborn's diet.

Myth: Hospitals, OB's, and doctors are well known for respecting patients' rights and choices. *Truth*: According to many different medical associations own internal documents, most policies are that consent is not needed for pretty much anything. I wrote an article for *Whole Woman Magazine* that explains how consent in hospitals is a polite illusion.

Myth: Lay midwives have no training. *Truth*: There are many midwifery training programs out there, and lay midwives are very popular in some areas. Ask each midwife that you interview what her training consisted of.

Myth: Home births are dangerous. Truth: There is no statistical evidence to support that claim.

Miscarriages

About one out of five pregnancies end in miscarriage. Many men have trouble grasping the reality of the pregnancy until they feel a kick, hear a heartbeat, or see a sonogram.   Due to this, some fathers do not understand the loss of an early pregnancy, no matter the type or time. A very gross analogy would be that for many fathers, they may see it as simply like losing an appendage. Men do not understand that at conception, there are powerful emotional, spiritual, physical, psychological, mental, and hormonal changes that occur in a woman.

Doulas

Doulas are the modern equivalent of women attendants of the past. My personal stance is they can be very useful. The father knows the mother better, the doula knows the birth story better. Together they can form a formidable team. Some confusion may come from the re-introduction of an old role (the woman attendant) with the introduction of an unestablished role (the father). Based on my historical research, I believe doulas came about to fill the gap of women as friends and family attending as a socio-spiritual event, not to replace the father. In that spirit, I think that doulas, family, and friends are good idea.

As for the origin of the term, in Henci Goer says this:

"Perhaps the most complicated thing about this new profession is the terminology. Dana Raphael first popularized the term doula, a Greek word meaning "woman caregiver," in her 1973 book, The Tender Gift. She used it to describe women who provided help and support to women after childbirth. Drs. Marshall Klaus and John Kennell adopted the term in the first of their studies, but they meant a labor support companion. Today, women who offer postpartum home-care services and women who do labor support both call themselves doulas, and some women do both. Polly Perez and Cheryl Snedecker, authors of *Special Women*, first published in 1990, distinguished between a *monitrice* and a doula. A monitrice has medical skills to monitor mother and baby and assess labor progress. *Birth assistant, childbirth assistant*, and *labor assistant* have all been used as synonyms for *doula* but may also be used to describe a midwife's assistant. I will use the term *doula*."[72] Author's italics.

C-sections

+ There are such things as Elective Cesareans. These are when the mother or the OB schedules a C-section in advance, on a planned date and time.
+ There are no standards for how or where the incision should be made on the uterus. It is stunning to research just how many different types of incisions are used.
+ A Special Scar has become a popular term for the unusual C-section incisions, such as Classical, Inverted T, Upright T, J, and also includes scars from other uterine surgeries such as a Myomectomy or a uterine rupture.[73]
+ The World Health Organization has said that the C-section rate should be around 10-15% for births. Although they removed that recommendation in 2010, they did not offer a new percentage.
+ The rate of C-sections in America is around 34%, around 24% in the United Kingdom, and around 30% in Australia.
+ The average for risk of serious complications for all cesareans is around 10.4%.[74]
+ The rate of complications during or after a scheduled cesarean is about 7.1%.[75]

---

[72] Goer, *The Thinking Woman's Guide to a Better Birth*, 178
[73] Special Scars ~ Special Women, http://www.specialscars.org
[74] Dr. Jen Gunter, "What is the rate of serious complications with a C-section?" Dr. Jen Gunter (blog), July 17, 2011, http://drjengunter.wordpress.com/2011/07/17/what-is-the-rate-of-serious-complications-with-a-c-section/
[75] See last footnote.

- VBACs are becoming increasingly more popular, for various reasons.

Chapter Eleven
Dear Thales

I suppose you are wondering why I am writing this. Well, it is a practice run. Throughout this book I spoke many times about how fathers don't talk to their sons about birth. I thought that I could lead the way and make an attempt here. You are only three years old at the time of this writing and have even sat on my lap a few times while writing this, but I hope you will read this many times when you are older. I'm taking the first step in establishing dialogue about childbirth between fathers and sons. I hope that what I'm doing now will not only help you, but set an example for other fathers to talk to their sons.

First of all, I have not included your sister Thalea in this speech. There are two reasons for that. First, your mother is training to be a midwife. There will be plenty for those two to talk about. Second, you are my son and therefore it is my duty as a father to prepare you for anything that you may encounter in life - which definitely could include birth. That's not to say that your mother won't have advice for you that you can only receive from a woman and her point of view, and the same goes for Thalea and I.

I don't know if you're going to want to go to college. You may want to learn how to do an oil change. You may decide to ask me to help you practice sports. I do know that you will pay taxes. It is a safe bet that you will get married. If I had to pick five things that I knew you were going to do in life, they would be: date people, pay taxes, get married, have kids, and buy or rent a place to live. I will give you advice and help you with any of those things.

Of the five things that I just listed, you can find ready and available advice on all those things except one. In our culture, fathers normally do not talk to their sons about the issue of pregnancy, and especially birth. I had to drag this information out of my father and grandfather. It caught them completely off guard when I asked, and I did not get much useful information.

What I learned from my grandfather was that my aunts and uncles were born during a time in American history when fathers were totally excluded from the delivery room. For his first four births, he paced in the hallway. He laughingly told me about how they had to wake him up in the hallway for the last birth in his family.

What I learned from my father was that he was one of the first of his generation to be allowed in the delivery room during the births of my brother and myself. By today's standards he would have been classified as a labor coach. When my father did talk to me about these births, he did not speak of it as a scary and emotional event. He spoke of it fondly, calmly, and rationally.

Which brings us to the next link in the chain: the births of you and your sister. Thalea's birth was a learning experience. I discovered many things during her birth, but the most important thing I learned was that I didn't know jack shit. It is always easier to analyze oneself in retrospect. I hope to save you that trouble.

For Thalea's birth, I wished I had lavished your mom with more options and services, not just money or objects, but physical services. Thalea was born at a freestanding birth center with a midwife helping us. I would have liked to have had more herbs, some incense, had a music CD prepped, and more of a homecoming with friends and family helping. A full opera producer approach with a green room for other players and an after show party are just a few of the things I wish I had arranged for.

For your birth, I guess I could say that I was aware of how unprepared I was. Your birth was unassisted. It was your mother, me, a doula who also happened to be a good friend, and the rest of our family at home. Your mother did her best to supply me with all the resources that I would need beforehand. For obvious reasons, they weren't enough, hence this book. I'm getting off track.

To be fair, in retrospect, there's not much that I would change for your birth. The double edged sword is that I felt that I did everything I could at the time but I still do not feel that I did everything that any father could do. It is hard to explain that many people consider what I did at your birth slightly remarkable. I look at it as doing the minimum of what all fathers should do.

We have your birth on video. You should do the same and record your children's births. As we get older we can go over the video, discuss birth plans, etc. (Don't worry, the video is not too gross.) You should do the same for your children.

In the strict terms of this book, for Thalea's birth, I was an opera producer. For your birth, I was a stage manager. What I wished I had been for both births was the Jean Baptiste Lully. However these are more fun musings than actual advice. This book is not about all the things that I would have done differently if I had the proper resources. What I am telling you is what I learned in that process.

You, and all sons out there, need and deserve all of the advice and wisdom that us fathers can give you.

This is not a one-time offer. You can always come to your mother or I for advice on birth at any time. This is something that I would gladly talk to you about at any age.

Perhaps the most important piece of advice that I could give you is – do not, I repeat, do not wait until you are married, or your wife is pregnant, to read a book or two on pregnancy and birth. People will read books and talk to other people before they buy a house or go to college. Why not take the same time to prepare for something that is pretty serious like pregnancy and birth?

There are a few positive outcomes from doing that. If the girl that you wish to marry finds out that you have already read one or two books on pregnancy and birth, that fact alone may be erase any doubts she has about you being a suitable husband. Another bonus is that you will be much less stressed if you do not have to worry about cramming as much information as you can about the subject in six months.

Reading about pregnancy and birth during pregnancy is like fixing a car while you are driving it. It is insane. By the time you finish it you will have missed half the stuff you are supposed to be preparing for. It makes more sense to read a pregnancy book when you decide to want to have children at any point your life, as long as it's well before the pregnancy.

Ignore what you see in movies and TV. They imply that you are some crude teenager throughout your life until you have a child and then, bam, you're magically an adult; but only after you resist some weird transformation. It is OK to dwell on the fact that all people change throughout their life and that seeing your child for the first time will be an extremely emotional event that will change you. It doesn't mean that you were a child or less of a man before the birth. Be yourself, set the example, let art reflect you.

On a side note, ignore what you see on TV about how mothers also act during and after labor. While writing this book I watched a show where a mother comes outside just hours after giving birth. She walks normally and also happens to shoot a man point blank with a huge revolver. The hours old baby she is holding doesn't make a peep when it hears a gunshot a few feet from its head. I hope your future wife won't want to have firearms at her birth. If so, chances are you will have plenty of experiences to write your own book.

Do not be afraid of couvade symptoms. The few you may get are fun to watch and usually go away. If you are unsure if what you are experiencing is in fact part of a couvade reaction, just call me or your mother.

Do not be intimidated by birth methods. Even at the time of this book there were over a dozen to choose from. This is going to upset a lot of people when they read this, but just like religion, I feel that no method was truly better than the other. They all have pros and cons. Treat them like a salad bar; pick and choose what you like about each one and develop your own philosophy based on you and your wife's unique personalities.

When you decide to read about the different birth methods there are keywords to look for when determining if a book reinforces the Medical Technocracy. If the book has these words: flexible, class or classes, father as defender, father as manager or coach, alternative, father as representative, natural, protection, father as warrior, method, nature, nurse midwife - don't read too much into it. Books with these keywords are usually just variations of a few other authors like Bradley and Dick-Read.

Hopefully, growing up around your mother and I, you will not need to read much. Having said that, if you do decide to read a guidebook for fathers there are tons of birth and pregnancy guides written by other fathers out there. Let me tell you that authors are human beings too, with all the same flaws as others. Some birth books out there suck hard. Your wife may have the best intentions when she asks you to read a few birth books. She may not know that they are some of the books that suck. Talk to me or your mother about what to read. It's not about reading tons of books; it's about reading the right one. A good father only needs to read one good book on pregnancy and birth, as it is just the first step on a long journey of talking and exploration with your pregnant wife.

The Internet has lots of random birth stories and blogs for or by fathers. Most are good but are too scattered in obscure places to do much good.

If you ever get the chance to go to someone else's birth before your own do it. Being around the birth atmosphere is quite intense, and birthing videos just don't come close to the real thing. Think of birth like a wedding. You go to others' weddings before your own. When the time comes for your own wedding, you have somewhat of a feeling of how it is supposed to go. Granted weddings and births are like apples and five-course Italian dinners, but seeing one beforehand never hurts in either case. Buy a birth DVD, like Gloria Lemay's *Birth*, if you can't attend another person's birth before your own partner's or watch your mother's copy.

Don't worry about money. Our society has lots of resources now between the Internet, friends, family, grandparents, diaper parties, baby showers, hand me downs, breastfeeding, cloth diapers, etc. I am not saying that it's ok to have nine children while you are living in our basement. I am saying that some people take their current financial situation a little too seriously when considering having children.

If your wife chooses to breastfeed, make yourself a good friend to the La Leche League. It may end up saving you a lot of energy. Be very encouraging of breastfeeding early on in the pregnancy.

Don't take hospital birthing classes. They just teach you how to be the perfect patient and to acquiesce to the real people who hold the power, the hospital.

If by that 1 in 100 chance you do have to have the entire birth in a hospital, totally ignore every piece of technology in the room. All they do is tell you what is going on with the mother, less accurately than the mother herself, who is more than capable of telling you what is going on with her.

Don't let anyone, family member, doctor, whoever, try to tell you what you and other fathers are supposed to be doing during birth. If someone does try to force their dogma on you, just ask that person what fathers were doing during births in Ancient Greece, or Medieval Europe, or even current indigenous societies for that matter. If the huge scope of history has taught us anything, fathers have run the gauntlet from totally there to completely absent. There is no true historical consensus. You do what feels right for you and your wife.

Midwives. What I am about to tell will be considered controversial by many people. When I say get a good midwife, I have to clarify. Things may be different by the time you are old enough to have kids, but as of right now, the midwife situation is pretty complicated. There is a difference between certified nurse midwives (CNMs) and lay midwives. To put it bluntly, CNM's are obstetrician assistants, and they usually have to work within and reinforce the hospital technocracy. Some know they are doing it, some try to oppose it, but the fact remains that they are working within the medical model.

Almost all lay midwives do not work within the medical model. Your wife may want a lay midwife. Depending on your state's laws, CNM's rarely do third party locale or home births. Lay midwives do. They may be hard to find, and interviewing them can be tedious, but it will be well worth it in the end.

Doulas. Do not underestimate this resource. Even if you are the most well-read of husbands and are an expert on childbirth, love your wife to the utmost; you are still not a woman. Throughout history laboring women have almost always had other women around them for support. For reasons we won't get into that trend fell by the wayside in the last century but is now undergoing a resurgence.

It will only be helpful for you, in any capacity that you choose for your wife's birth, to have other women around that she trusts for company and assistance. No matter how much you know, you cannot have the physical empathy that other women offer. Don't let that get you down though because none of those women are your wife's husband. There's only one of you and that makes you vitally important to her. I hope that you use this resource wisely.

On the flip side, make sure that this doula will not just shove you to the side. There are some doulas out there who are not good, like any other profession. I have heard of doulas that shove the father aside as if he knew nothing and think they should sit in the corner quietly. It is rare as most doulas know that they are there to support both parents. Also do not let you or your wife wait until late in the pregnancy to choose a doula. If you haven't shopped around before the pregnancy, be sure to have one chosen as soon as possible after conception is known. Doulas can also help you find a good midwife.

Paperwork. The trick to not getting overwhelmed with paperwork involved in birth is to study and become familiar with the right ones. You don't have to know about every form or chart associated with birth. I will tell you about the important ones. Birth plans should be the most important form you should focus on. Others may include Apgar Tests, Partograms, and Bishop Scores. Develop your own birth plan. It is very easy to search around and find a good cross section of short vs. detailed birth plans.

Being pro-vbac and pro-home birth does not mean that one is anti-hospital or anti C-section. Hospitals and C-sections do have their purposes and times but they can't be the automatic response to all births. Trying to present any side as an absolute truth only shows that person as having an agenda. This confuses expecting parents while preventing progress. Don't fall into that type of thinking.

There is a very small chance that your wife will have to have a legitimate C-section. And I mean very small chance, probably less than 10%. If she does have one, it will change things significantly for you, the mother, and the baby. The chances of your loved one having emotional concerns after a C-section are increased so you will have to be even more supportive than normal.

I don't want to scare you, but surgery by itself is quite an ordeal for some people. I talked with an anesthesiologist once and he said most people are very nervous before they get knocked out for a normal surgery. Now add to that anxiety the knowledge that there is a complication with the infant or her, which only adds hugely to the already present anxiety. There is nothing I could say or describe that would do justice to what mothers feel before, during, and after a C-section. What I can do is tell you that it is an extraordinary circumstance that will require extraordinary understanding and support from you.

Another important thing to remember about C-sections is that no matter who says what, women after surgery heal like everyone else. Treat your loved one as healed and normal until someone can prove without a doubt otherwise. Be highly skeptical of anyone who says that she can't have another birth normally.

I could talk with you at length about the different definitions and levels of baby blues and postpartum depression. It would be much easier for you if I just told you to do everything for the first two weeks after the birth. After the birth, the only thing your wife should have to do for at least two weeks is sleep, eat, and feed the baby. Everything else, *everything,* you should be doing. If the mother wants to do a menial chore here and there to break the routine and move around, then by all means, let her.

When it comes to birth trauma even the best laid plans can go awry. If the mother of your child happens to experience birth trauma - acknowledgement is half the battle. No one expects you to sweep away the pain in one conversation. It can take years so be patient. What happens after the acknowledgement depends on the intricacies of the relationship between you and the mother.

Don't be an idiot and force her to do nothing for two weeks. The important thing is for her to know that she doesn't have to do much if she doesn't want to. Recovery from birth requires many types of healing: physical, emotional, spiritual, hormonal, self-esteem, etc. Time and rest are the best healers for all those things.

Here are a few other help tips that some other mothers wanted me to tell you. It is perfectly acceptable to use a rolling pin with cloth or an ice pack on it for massage during labor. Freeze a lot of washcloths before the birth, they can be heaven on the forehead during labor. If you are giving your wife ice chips during labor, you need to know that it's hard for her to hold a cup during contractions. Take breath mints.

I'd recommend that during the pregnancy you talk to your expectant wife at least once a day. She may have changed her mind about some things, decided against others, etc. The more you know her mind about every little detail leading up to the birth, the smoother the labor and birth will go and the more you will be able to help her.

The only rule is there is an exception to every rule. Look for social rules, be that exception... in regards to birth.

Birth stools and pools are awesome. Shop around early for those two birth accessories.

An expert on the subject, Richard Reed, said that birth was not irrational, it is non-rational. Never forget that. Throughout all of my research and readings that is one of the phrases that really stuck with me.

Just as the work of an engineer or architect is more than cutting the tape and entering a finished building, the work of a father at birth is more than cutting the cord and catching the baby.

I hope you have fun choosing one of my roles, and making it five times better.

The birthing hour holds that magical moment when your baby is born. It is when your identity and choice of role for that moment is forged together in the crucible of birth. You will carry that identity with you for the rest of your life.

And lastly, talk with your children often, as I will talk with you.

Bibliography

Books

Balaskas, Janet. *Active Birth: The New Approach to Giving Birth Naturally*. Harvard: The Harvard Common Press, 1992.

Barron, James Douglas. *She's Having a Baby - and I'm Having a Breakdown*. New York: Quill, William Morrow and Company, 1998.

Bishop, Greg. *A Crash Course for New Dads*. Irvine: Dads Adventure, Inc., 2008

Block, Polly. *Polly's Birth Book*. American Fork: Hearthspun Publishers, 1984.

Bradley, Robert A. *Husband Coached Childbirth,* rev. ed. New York: Harper and Row, Publisher, 1974.

Brott, Armin A, and Jennifer Ash. *The Expectant Father*. New York: Abbeville Press Publishers, 2001.

Brott, Armin A. *Father for Life: A Journey of Joy, Challenge, and Change*. New York: Abbeville Press Publishers, 2003.

Cortlund, Yana, Barb Lucke, and Donna Miller Watelet. *Mother Rising: The Blessingway Journey into Motherhood*. Berkeley: Celestial Arts, 2006.

Cosby, Bill. *Fatherhood*. New York: Berkley Books, 1986.

Crider, Michael. *The Guy's Guide to Surviving Pregnancy, Childbirth, and the First Year of Fatherhood*. Cambridge: Da Capo Press, 2005.

Curtis, Glade B., MD, and Judith Schuler. *Your Pregnancy: For the Father-To-Be*. Philadelphia: Da Capo Press, 2009.

Davis, Ian. *My Boys Can Swim! The Official Guy's Guide to Pregnancy*. Roseville: Prima Publishing, 1999.

Dick-Read, Grantly. *Childbirth Without Fear*. 2nd rev. ed. New York: Harper & Brothers, 1944.

Downey, Peter. *So You're Going to Be a Dad*. Cambridge: Da Capo Press, 2000.

Dundes, Lauren, ed. *The Manner Born: Birth Rites in Cross-Cultural Perspective*. Walnut Creek: Altamira Press, 2003.

Enning, Cornelia. *Placenta: The Gift of Life*. Eugene: Motherbaby Press, 2007.

Fielding, Henry. *Amelia*. Edited by Linda Bree. Ontario: Broadview Press, 2010. First published 1751 by Andrew Miller.

Flaceliere, Robert. *Daily Life in Greece at the Time of Pericles*. London: Phoenix Publishing, 1965.

Gaskin, Ina May. *Spiritual Midwifery*. rev. ed. Summertown: The Book Publishing Company, 1977.

Goer, Henci. *The Thinking Woman's Guide to a Better Birth*. New York: Perigree, 1999.

Hazard, Leah. *The Father's Home Birth Handbook*. London: Pinter and Martin Ltd., 2010.

Houser, Patrick M. *Fathers-To-Be Handbook*. South Portland: Creative Life Systems, 2009.

Karmel, Marjorie, and Alex Karmel. *Thank You, Dr. Lamaze.* London: Pinter & Martin, Ltd., 2005

Kimes, Joanne, and Jeff Kimes. *Pregnancy Sucks for Men.* Avon: Adams Media, 2004.

Kitzinger, Sheila. *The Complete Book of Pregnancy and Childbirth.* 4th ed. New York: Alfred A. Knopf, 2005.

Leavitt, Judith Walzer. *Make Room for Daddy: The Journey from Waiting Room to Birthing Room.* Chapel Hill: The University of North Carolina Press, 2009.

Leboyer, Frederick. *Birth Without Violence.* New York: Alfred A. Knopf, 1975.

Lewis-Stempel, John, ed. *Fatherhood: An Anthology.* Woodstock: The Overlook Press, 2003.

Lloyd, Bill, and Scott Finch. *The Dude's Guide to Pregnancy: Dealing with Your Expecting Wife, Coming Baby, and the End of Life as You Knew It.* New York: Wellness Central, 2008.

Mactavish, Scott. *The New Dad's Survival Guide.* New York: Little, Brown, and Company, 2005.

Mander, Rosemary. *Men and Maternity.* New York: Routledge Taylor and Francis Group, 2004.

McCutcheon, Susan. *Natural Childbirth the Bradley Way.* rev. New York: Penguin Group, 1996.

Mongan, Marie F., M.Ed., M.Hy. *HypnoBirthing, The Mongan Method.* 3rd ed. Deerfield Beach: Health Communications Inc., 2005.

Nevius, C.W. *Crouching Father, Hidden Toddler: A Zen Guide for New Dads*. San Francisco: Chronicle Books, 2006.

Odent, Michel. *Birth Reborn*. New York: Pantheon Books, 1984.

———. *Birth and Breastfeeding*. Forest Row: Clairview Books, 2003.

Port, David, and John Ralston. *The Caveman's Pregnancy Companion: A Survival Guide for Expectant Fathers*. New York: Sterling Publishing Co., Inc., 2006.

Powell, Barry B. *Classical Myth*. New Jersey: Pearson Prentice Hall, 2004.

Reed, Richard K. *Birthing Fathers: The Transformation of Men in American Rites of Birth*. New Brunswick: Rutgers University Press, 2005.

Reynalde, Thomas. *The Birth of Mankind: Otherwise Named the Woman's Book*. Edited by Elaine Hobby. 1560. Reprint, Surrey: Ashgate Publishing Limited, 2009.

Simkin, Penny, Janet Whalley, and Ann Keppler. *Pregnancy, Childbirth, and the Newborn: The Complete Guide*. New York: Meadowbrook Press, 2001.

Simkin, Penny. *The Birth Partner: A Complete Guide to Childbirth for Dads, Doulas, and All Other Labor Companions*. 3rd ed. Boston: Harvard Common Press, 2008.

Soranus. *Gynecology*. Translated by Owsei Temkin, MD. Baltimore: Johns Hopkins University Press, 1991.

Spacek, Tim. *Fathers: There at the Birth*. Chicago: Chicago Review Press, 1985.

Squire, Caroline, ed. *The Social Context of Birth.* Oxford: Radcliffe Publishing, 2009.

St. John, Rose. *Fathers at Birth.* Portland: Ringing Bell Press, 2009.

Stedman's Medical Dictionary. 7th ed. Philadelphia: Lippincott, Williams & Wilkins, 2012.

Stubbs, Sheila. *Birthing the Easy Way.* Springford: Self-Published, 2008.

Sweet, O. Robin, and Patty Bryan. *The Working Woman's Lamaze Handbook.* New York: Hyperion, 1992.

Taber's Cyclopedic Medical Dictionary. 21st ed. Philadelphia: F.A. Davis Company, 2005.

Thicke, Alan. *How Men Have Babies: The Pregnant Father's Survival Guide.* Chicago: Contemporary Books, 1998.

Tosh, John. *A Man's Place: Masculinity and Middle Class Home in Victorian England.* New Haven: Yale University Press, 1999.

Worsley, Lucy. *If Walls Could Talk, An Intimate History of the Home.* New York: Walker and Company, 2011.

Movies

Apatow, Judd. *Knocked Up.* DVD. Directed by Judd Apatow. California: Universal Pictures, 2007.

Braoude, Patrick, Chris Columbus. *Nine Months.* DVD. Directed by Chris Columbus. Los Angeles, CA: Twentieth Century Fox Film Corporation, 1995.

Cody, Diablo. *Juno.* DVD. Directed by Jason Reitman. Hollywood, Los Angeles, CA: Fox Searchlight Pictures, 2007.

Ganz, Lowell, Billie Letts, Babaloo Mendel. *Where the Heart Is*. DVD. Directed by Matt Williams. Los Angeles, CA: Twentieth Century Fox Film Corporation, 2000.

Hackett, Albert, Frances Goodrich, Nancy Meyers, Charles Shyer. *Father of the Bride, Part II*. DVD. Directed by Charles Shyer. Pilot Mountain, NC: Sandollar Productions, 1995.

Hughes, John. *National Lampoon's Christmas Vacation*. DVD. Directed by Jeremiah S. Chechik. Hollywood, Los Angeles, CA: Warner Bros., 1989.

———. *She's Having a Baby*. DVD. Directed by John Hughes. Los Angeles, CA: Hughes Entertainment, Paramount Pictures, 1988.

Lemay, Gloria. *Birth*. DVD. Canada, 2010

Levin, Ira, Roman Polanski. *Rosemary's Baby*. DVD. Directed by Roman Polanski. Hollywood, Los Angeles, CA: William Castle Productions, 1968.